D1830862

OUTLINE GRAMMAR

OF THE

GARO LANGUAGE

Owing to the antiquity and rarity of this book, certain pages are regrettably absent, and readability is compromised due to the blurring of the original text. If you possess any insights regarding the availability of these missing sections, kindly inform us. Your assistance is crucial in ensuring the completion of this significant work for the benefit of future generations.

OUTLINE GRAMMAR

OF THE

GARO LANGUAGE

T. J. KEITH

GYAN

Published by

Gyan Publishing House
5, Ansari Road
Daryaganj, New Delhi-110002
Phone: 011-47034999, 9811692060
E-mail: books@gyanbooks.com

Distribution Network
gyanbooks.com
India, USA, Canada, UK, Australia

© Publisher

All rights reserved. No part of this work may be reproduced, stored, adapted, or transmitted in any form or by any means, electronic, mechanical, photocopying, micro-filming, recording or otherwise, or translated in any language, without the prior written permission of the copyright owner and the publisher.

ISBN: 978-93-6780-135-2 (HB)

First Published, 1874

2nd Impression 2024

Printed at: Gyan Press, Delhi.

The book is sold subject to the condition that it shall not, by way of trade or otherwise, be lent, resold, hired out, or otherwise circulated without the prior publisher's written consent.

OUTLINE GRAMMAR OF THE GARO LANGUAGE
Author: T. J. KEITH

OUTLINE GRAMMAR

OF THE

GARO LANGUAGE

BY

T. J. KEITH

AMERICAN MISSIONARY.

SIBSAGOR

BAPTIST MISSION PRESS

1874.

PREFACE.

To find the place of the Garo dialect in the great family of languages is not easy. In its grammatical construction it has not a few points of resemblance to the Sanskrit and her numerous offspring.

Starting with the Pers. Pro. First Pers., we have in Sanskrit, *aham* or *ahang,* in Bengali *ámi* and in Garo *ángá, I.*

Also, Plural number Poss. Case, Sans., *ashakam,* Bengali, *amaddre,* and Garo, *achhingni, Ours.*

Again the Rel. Pro. Sanskrit Mas. Gender is *jah,* Fem. *ja;* in Bengali *jé* and *jaha;* Hindustani *jo,* and in Garo *jé, he or she whom, or that which.*

Also in the manner of denoting the cases of nouns, and pronouns, the Garo resembles the Aryan family of tongues. As, in all those languages, the case denoting word (called in English a preposition,) is an affix joined to the word whose case it indicates, so also in Garo.

Resemblance is still further seen in the Nom. Case having no affix.

Comparing the case affixes, we find that in the Objective case at least, the Garo bears some relation to the Bengali and Hindustani; as, Beng. *tumaké,* Hind. *tumko,* Garo *Nang-kho.*

The sign of the Infinitive Mood is the same in Garo and Hindustani. As Hind. *mar-na,* to strike, Garo *dak-na, to strike;* Hind. *dekh-na, to see,* Garo *nik-na, to see.*

Again in the "Comparison of adjectives," there is a striking similarity between the Garo and the Sanskritic languages. That is, in not changing the form of the adjective to express degrees of comparison, as in English, but accomplishing this by connecting one object with another with a word equivalent to *than* in English and expressing the degree of comparison by the adjective. The following example will illustrate the rule.

Eng., "This house is higher than that."

Hind., "*Us gharse yih ghar buland hai.*"

Beng., *Shé ghar hoité ai ghar uchha (asé)*

Garo, *Ua nokna bate ia nok chubata.*

Eng., lit. *That house than this house high is.*

The same resemblance is carried out in the superlative degree.

Still another striking point of resemblance is seen in the method of connecting a subordinate member of a sentence with the next following verb having the same agent and in this way avoiding the necessity of connective conjunctions. As a familiar example of this take the following,—

Eng., *take him away.*

Hind., *usko lé jao.*

Beng., *tahaké niya jaeo.*

Garo, *uákho raé iyangbo,* contract form *raangbo.*

In each language the principle is the same, i. e. the indefinite participle, *having taken* is first expressed and connected immediately with the verb of direct action, as, *having taken*, (him) *go*. In the same way.,—

Hind., *yih kam ko kurké giya.*

Beng., *ei kam kariya giyasé.*

Garo, *iya khamkho khayé iyangjok.*

Eng., *this work having done went.* Properly, "*having performed the work he departed.*" Many other points of resemblance might be pointed out between the Garo and the Sanskritic languages. But these are sufficient to awaken the interesting inquiry as to how these languages came to have so much similarity in their grammatical construction, when after all, tried by definition of words they are utterly unlike and different.

Take any of the words denoting the family relations, names of the common and domestic animals, of places of abode, of cooking implements and of agricultural terms and all attempts to trace resemblance fail entirely.

Turning then from the Sanskrit derivitives where among the aboriginal languages of India belongs the Garo? Out of 57 brief comparative vocabularies compiled by Col. Dalton, (see, Ethnology of Bengal,) there are five dialects with which the Garo has words in common or nearly so. These dialects are, the Chutia, the Kachari, the Dhimal, the Mech and the Kooch. But of these the Kachari presents the greatest number of words that are also found in the Garo. Thus,—

Kachari	gni	Garo	gni	Eng.	two
,,	tham	,,	githam	,,	three
,,	bri	,,	bri	,,	four
,,	baa	,,	banga	,,	five
,,	dau	,,	dauk	,,	six
,,	chhni	,,	sni	,,	seven
,,	ang	,,	anga	,,	I
,,	nang	,,	naa	,,	you
,,	janga	,,	chinga	,,	we
,,	angni	,,	angni	,,	of me
,,	nangni	,,	nangni	,,	of you
,,	gungthung	,,	gingthing	,,	nose
,,	mogou	,,	mikrou	,,	eye
,,	khonga	,,	kushik	,,	mouth
,,	khoro	,,	skho	,,	head
,,	shlé	,,	sré	,,	tongue
,,	apha	,,	apha	,,	father
,,	bida	,,	ada	,,	brother
,,	no	,,	angano	,,	sister
,,	manshi	,,	mandé	,,	man
,,	bisha	,,	bisha	,,	child.

These words alike, or nearly so as found in both languages, and taken in connection with a similarity in grammatical construction, especially in the case affixes, establish clearly a radical connection between the speech of the two races, the Garo and the Kachari. Beyond this, we are at present, unable to go. And it is chiefly with a view of aiding others who may have more ability and leisure for the task, in tracing up to their common source these dialects, and so far, to find the natural place of these scattered tribes and races in the great human family, that this brief analysis of the Garo tongue is written.

The writer must confess to numerous errors and inconsistencies, especially in the transliteration of Garo words. For these and all other errors, the only excuse that can be given is a multiplicity of diversified, and sometimes, distracting duties.

T. J. Keith.

Gowalpara Assam,
Dec. 24th 1874.

OUTLINE GARO GRAMMAR.

The following exposition of the leading principles of the Gáro language will be comprised in seven chapters, viz Orthography, Nouns, Pronouns, Adjectives, Verbs, Adverbs &c. and Miscellaneous Exercises.

CHAPTER I.

ORTHOGRAPHY.

This treats of the Alphabet as used in writing Garo, with the division, names, pronunciation and power of its letters.

Section First, The Alphabet.

The BENGALI Alphabet, as being used by people contiguous to the Garos on three sides, as being known by large numbers of the Garos themselves and as being adapted equally with any other for expressing the sounds of Garo words, has been chosen as the best for writing the language. The Bengáli Alphabet is as follows;

ALPHABET.

Vowels.

a	áh	i	i
অ	আ	ই	ঈ
u	ú	ri	rí
উ	ঊ	ঋ	ৠ
lri	lrí	e	ai
ঌ	ৡ	এ	ঐ
o	au	ang	ah
ও	ঔ	অং	অঃ

Consonants.

ka	kha	ga	gha	ynua
ক	খ	গ	ঘ	ঙ
cha	chha	ja	jha	gnia
চ	ছ	জ	ঝ	ঞ
ta	tha	da	dha	ana
ট	ঠ	ড	ঢ	ণ
ta	tha	da	dha	na
ত	থ	দ	ধ	ন

pa	pha	ba	bha	ma
প	ফ	ব	ভ	ম
ja	**ra**	**la**	**va**	**sha**
য	র	ল	ব	শ
sha	**sa**	**ha**	**khya**	
ষ	স	হ	ক্ষ ।	

The foregoing comprises the whole alphabet as used in the Bengáli language; but as the Garo language has not been under critical study long enough to develop all the nice distinctions of sounds indicated by the whole 51 letters in the Bengáli alphabet, a less number of characters has been found sufficient for practical purposes in expressing it; thus,

Bengali Alphabet as used in writing Garo.

Vowels, (Swar.)

a	áh	i	u
অ	আ	ই	উ
e	**o**	**ang**	**ah**
এ	ও	অং	অঃ

Consonants, (Byanjan.)

ka ক	kha খ	ga গ	cha চ
chha ছ	ja jha জ	ta ত	tha থ
da দ	na ন	pa প	pha ফ
b, or va ব	ma ম	ya য়	ra র
la ল	sha শ	sa স	ha হ

Section Second, Pronunciation of Letters.

The pronunciation of the letters follows the same rule substantially, as in the Bengali alphabet.

অ *a*, the first vowel is supposed to belong to every consonant, which is not accompanied by another vowel, and is pronounced with it. Its sound is that of *a* in *fall* or *hawk.* thus অন্না *anná, to give.*

আ *á* this is the long form of the above letter. Its sound is that of *a* in *father;* as আমাক *ámák*, a monkey.

ই *i*, this letter is pronounced as *i* in *tin* and as *e* in such words as *been, he* &c. It is also used to indicate a *half vowel* sound which is often heard in Garo, as ইন্না *enná, to speak, to tell.*

উ *u*, has the sound of *u* in *truth.* উয়া *uá, he*

এ *e*, this letter is pronounced as *e* in *prey* and *where* as একা *eká, to divide.*

ও *o*, like *o* in *note* as ওয়াক *owák, a hog.*

ং "*ng*" this character represents the sound of "*ng.*" It is made great use of in Garo. It is not found as the *initial* sound of a word but often occurs in connection with other full vowel sounds, as অংআ *angá, state, condition.*

"ঃ" *ah*, this letter is used to represent a sound some what difficult to describe but which is often heard among the Garos as among most of the hill people of India. It seems to be caused by the sound being suddenly shut off in, or at the entrance to the nasal passages, producing a short, jerking, broken utterance. It is an exaggeration of the Bengali pronunciation of the *bisarga*, as আঃআ *áh-áh, earth.*

ক *ka*, this consonant is pronounced as *k* in *kind, king*, &c. It never occurs in the Garo language as the *initial* of a word.

খ *kh*, has the sound of *kh*, as *kha*, thus খংআ *khanga to dig.*

গ *ga*, has the sound of *g* hard as in *gain* thus গআ, *gaáh, to throw.*

চ *cha*, has the sound of "*ch*," as in *chance*, চআ *chaá to row*.

ছ *chha, chh* as *ch-h* in *much haste*. This letter is not used as the initial in Garo words, the above written চ being considered sufficient to represent the class of sounds which this letter represents in the Bengali.

জ *ja*, this letter, which has the sound of *j* in English, like the foregoing, is used to represent all those sounds in Garo for which জ, ঝ, য are used in Bengali. It is pronounced as *j* in *James*, thus জামান *jámán, after*.

ত *ta*, this letter in like *t* in *teeth*, as গিতা *gitá, like.* It never occurs as the initial consonant of a word in Garo.

থ *tha*, this is "*th*," as in *thus*, as থআ *thaá, to weigh*.

The two foregoing letters supply the place, in Garo of the four letters, ট, ঠ, ত and থ in Bengali.

দ *da*, this letter is pronounced as *d* in *door* thus দংআ *dangá, to be*, or *to remain*.

ন *na*, this is simply *n* as in *not, nod* &c. thus নক্ nak a *house*.

প *pa*, this letter like *p* in *pen*. It does not occur as an *initial* letter.

ফ *pha*, this character answers the purpose in Garo of both প and ফ in Bengali as an *initial* letter. Its pronunciation however differs slighly from either of them. It is not the clear explosive sound of *p* as in *pin* and of প as in পান, neither of *ph* as in *physic* and of ফ as in ফল but it represents a kind of explosive "*ph*" sound, thus ফালা *p-h-*(uttered together) *phálá to buy, to barter.*

ব *ba*, has the sound of *b* in *book, ball* &c. as বল *bal, a tree.*

ম *ma*, is pronounced as *m* in *man*, as মাআ, *mother.*

য় *ya*, this letter is equivaleat to *y* in English. It does not occur as the initial letter of a word in Garo, and is not used except after a vowel sound, thus উইয়া *uiyá, to know, to understand.*

র *ra*, in Garo is sounded as *r* in *rock*, as রঅং, *raang, a stone.*

ল *la*, this is like *l* in English. Singular to say the *l* sound is not heard as the *initial* sound of any word in Garo, the preference being given to র with its liquid sound, বল *bal, tree.*

স শ *sha*, these two letters have no appreciable difference of pronunciation as used in Garo and their use is more the result of habits formed in writing Bengali than from any necessity of the language. As they are both in general use however, it is not deemed best to throw either of them out of the alphabet. Their sound is that of *s* and *sh*, more generally that of the latter, as সং *shang, country* or *village.*

হ *ha*, has the sound of h in *hall*, as হাজাল *hájál, a thousand.*

Section Third, Union of Vowels with Consonants.

The union of vowels with consonants as also consonants with each other follow the same rules in general as in Bengali. Every consonant by itself is supposed to have the first vowel অ inherent in it, unless (্) *biram*' is written after it or another consonant is joined to it then the অ sound is dropped, only the consonant sound remaining, thus অক্ *not aka* but অক্ *ak.* If any other vowel is united to the consonant, it takes the place of অ as কে *ke.*

When vowels and consonants are joined, the original form of the vowel is dropped and the following symbols take their place.

অ	is left blank,		as	ক	ka
আ	becomes	(া)	as	কা	ká
ই		(ি)		কি	ki
উ		(ু)		কু	ku
এ		(ে)		কে	ké
ও		(ো)		কো	ko
অং		(ং)		কং	kang
অঃ		(ঃ)		কঃ	kh

Section Fourth, Union of Consonants.

In writing Garo, consonants are united in two ways.

1 The first is the common way of writing the one over the other, as ফ্লাক *phlák, all.*

In this way of writing consonants, usually ane or both letters undergo a change of form, thus, স্খো *skho, head,* আম্বল *ámbol, wood.*

2. The other, may be termed the *irregular* union of consonants. The union is chiefly that of the letter র with other consonants, and is usually written *below* as in the following, স্রে sré, *tongue*, মিক্রন, mikran; *eye* &c. Sometimes, however, this letter joins to উ in which case its form is thus ব্রুরুং búrúng, a *forest, jungle;* joined to ত its form is thus ত্র &c.

CHAPTER II.

Nouns.

To nouns, in Garo belong gender, number and case.

Section First, Of Gender.

Nouns are said to be of the masculine, feminine or neuter gender according to the character of the objects for which they stand, as মান্দে, mándé, *man*, মেচিক méchik, *woman*, নক, nak, *house.*

(1.) Masculine gender.—a. The masculine gender of rational beings is indicated by the name itself, used absolutely as মেয়া méá, *man*, আফা áphá, *father*, ফামুরি, phámuri, *a young man.*

b. The masculine gender of irrational animals is indicated by বিফা biphá, meaning *male*, thus দবক্ dabak *sheep*, দবক্ বিফা dabak biphá, *buck, ram.*

Note. This method of forming the masculine includes all living things without intelligence, such as birds, fish, reptiles as well as all beasts.

2. Feminine gender.—a. The feminine of all rational creatures is indicated usually by the name itself; as

মাআ máá, *mother*, জিক্ jik, *wife*, আংনো ángno, *sister*.

Excep. An exception is seen sometimes, however, when the noun is qualified by the word মেচিক্ méchik, meaning woman or, more strictly, *female* as, বিসা bisá *child, infant*, মেচিক্-বিসা mechik-bishá, *female infant, girl*.

b. The feminine gender of irrational animals is shown by the qualifying word বিমা bimá, meaning *female*, written after, thus আচাক áchák, *dog*, আচাক-বিমা áchák-bimá, *bitch*; দবক্ dabak, *sheep*, দবক্-বিমা, dabak-bimá, *ewe;* দো do, *a bird, fowl*, দো-বিমা do bimá, *a female bird*, a *hen*.

This method of indicating the feminine gender includes all living, irrational things.

3. Neuter gender.—In general, nouns which denote things without life have no gender; hence are neuter, as নক nak, *house*, সাল sál, *Sun* &c.

Excep. When however the inanimate object possesses or is supposed to possess some of the qualities of animate things, they are spoken of as though they had gender. Thus a tree which bears fruit, from its bearing quality, is spoken of as of the feminine gender and denoted by the sign of the irrational feminine, thus বল bal, *a tree, and* বল-বিমা bal-bimá, *a female tree*, i. e. a fruit bearing tree.

Section Second;—Of Number.

In Garo but two numbers are recognized, the singular and plural.

1. *Singular number.*—The singular number is indicated either by the single name of the object or by some word signifying *one,* as নক **nak,** *house,* রঅং raang, *stone,* মান্দে সাক্সা, **mándé shákshá,** *a man or one man.*

2. *Plural Number.*—The plurality of things is usually indicated by the affix রাং *ráng* to the singular, as মান্দে mándé, *man,* মান্দেরাং mándéráng, *men,* আচাক áchák, *a dog,* আচাকরাং áchákráng, *dogs.*

Note 1. The above plural affix is often changed for the sake of euphony into দ্রাং *dráng,* as বল bal, a *tree,* বলদ্রাং, bal-dráng, *trees &c.*

Note 2. Besides the above regular affixes, plurality is sometimes indicated by the adverbs দারাং dạráng, ফ্লাকান phlákán, জিন্‌মা jinmá &c, meaning *all, the whole* or *many, several &c.*

Note 3. When the definite number one or more is to be designated, the numeral adjectives are used, and usually written after the noun or word which they qualify, as মান্দে সাক্‌গ্নি mándé shákgni, *two men* মাচ্ছামাংগিথাম্ máccha máng githám, *three tigers,* ফায়সা' খাপ্‌বংআ pháshá kháp bangá, *five pice &c.*

Note 4. It will be observed that when number is thus designated a number of enclitic particles are used in conjunction with the adjective word.

These are, "*a,*" for human beings সাক *shák,* as মান্দে সাক্সা mánde shákshá, *one man;* মেচিক সাকগ্নি mechik shákgni, *two women,* বিসা সাক গিথাম, bishá shák githám, *three children. &c.*

"*b*" For irrational animals মাং *máng*, as মাচ্ছুমাংবংআ mácchu máng bangá, *five cows,* দোবিমামাং চেত্ dobimá máng chet, *ten cocks.* &c,

"*c*" For enumerating fruits and all *round* objects, রং is used. As থেব্রংরং গিথাম্ thebrong rong githam, *three jackapples,* দোচিরংবংআ dochi rang bangá, *five eggs,* &c.

"*d*" For pice and money in general খাপ, ফেল and গং are used. As ফায়সা খাপসা pháshá khapshá, *one pice,* ফায়সা ফেল গ্নি pháshá phél gni, *two pice,* থাংখা গংব্রি thángkhá gang bri, *four rupees.* &c.

"*e*" For things that are in pieces, such as boxes, tables, *kabarees* and such like, গে *ge,* is used, as খেরা-গে গিথাম্ kherá gé githám, *three baskets* &c.

"*f*" In counting leaves of trees or books or lessons, chapters, verses &c. জাক্ is used, as এসাল জাক্সা éshál jákshá, "*one leaf.*" These are perhaps the most important of these troublesome particles; but there are many others in the language; and applied in the same way, apparently arbitrary, not governed by *any* definite rules. They must be learned from constant practice in hearing and speaking.

Section Third;—Of Case.

In Garo, nouns may be distinguished in eight cases, viz, nominative, objective, instrumental, dative, ablative, possessive and locative.

1. Nominative case.—The noun in the nominative case is always the subject of a sentence and has no case ending. It is the simple form of the word in its original state, as, বিসা খাদিংআ bishá khádingá, *the child laughs,* বিসা *bisha* is nominative.

2. Objective case.—A noun is in the objective case when it denotes a person or thing upon which any action, as of seeing, hearing, tasting, bringing, striking &c, terminates.

In Garo this relation is designated by the affix খো *kho,* as আংআ রামসিংখো নিকা Angá Rámsingkho niká, "*I see Ramsing.*" ওমেদ থরংখো দকেংআ *Omed is striking* Thorong.

Note. In the case of nouns of the neuter gender when put in the objective case, the objective sign is sometimes, though rarely, omitted.

3. Instrumental case.—Nouns which denote objects that are the means, or instruments, through, or with which any thing is done are said to be in the instrumental case. In Garo this case is indicated by the affix চি *chi as* উয়া রুআচি সুআ uá ruáchi shuá, "*he cuts with an ax,*" রুআ-চি, *ruá-chi,* instrumental case.

4. Dative case.—Nouns which denote objects that are in the relation of *reception* are considered as in the dative case. This includes the reception of all objects given, as money, books, clothing, and also the moral qualities of love and hate &c. The termination of this case in Garo is না *ná.* as, নাআ. মংমানা সামখো অন্‌বো, náá mongmáná shámkho anbo, "*give (or you) give grass to the elephant,*" ইসল দারাং মান্দেনান খাসারা, Eshal dáráng mándénán kháshárá," "*God loves all men.*" মাংসা-

না, mángmáná, and দারাং মান্দেনান, dáráng mándenán, are in the dative case.

5. *Ablative case.*—Nouns which denote the place or source from which any thing comes or goes or is brought, are said to be in the ablative case; and are designated by two affixes ওনি, *oni*, and ওনিখো *onikho*, as নকোনি রেআংবো nakoni réángbo, "*go out of the house.*" আংআ বলোনিখো থেব্রং আকা angá balonikho thebrong áká, "*I take the jackapple from the tree.*"

Note. The rule for distinguishing the use of these two affixes is as follows, viz;—

1. When any person or thing is represented as issuing out from, or leaving any thing or place of his or its own accord or power, or without the agency of another, then the former or ওনি, *oni*, form is used as বলোনি বিথে গাআকা, baloni bithé gááká, "*fruit falls from the tree.*"

2. When any person or thing is represented as leaving any place by the agency of another, the affix ওনিখো *onikho*, is used, as, উয়া বলোনিখো বিথেখো আকা, uá balonikho bithékho áká, *he plucks fruit from the tree.*

6. *Possessive case.*—Words which designate objects that stand in the relation of origin or possession are said to be in the possessive case. In Garo, its sign is নি, *ni* as বিমানি চি bimáni chi "*the water of the river.*" মান্দেনি জাংগি mándéni jángi, "*the life of man.*" বিমানি, মান্দেনি, bimáni, mándeni, are possessive.

7. *Locative case.*—Those nouns that designate places which contain or receive any thing are said to be in the locative case. This relation in Garo is designated by three different affixes ও *o*, ওনা *oná*, চি চিনা *chi* or *chiná*. আচাক নকো গ্নাং áchák nako gnáng, *the dog is in the house.* সাহেব দামরাওনা রেগেন, sáheb damráoná regen, "*Sáheb will go to Damra.*" মাচ্ছা আব্রিচি রেআংআহা, mácchá ábrichi réángáhá, "*the tiger went into the mountain.*"

Note "a," Nouns which designate objects in which any thing *is* or *remains* take as their affix ও, *o*, as বিসা নকো দংআ, bisha nako dangá, "*the child is (or remains) in the house.*"

"*b*" Nouns which designate objects or places to or into which any thing goes or enters, take, sometimes ওনা *oná*, some times, চি *chi*, and some times, চিনা *chiná* as মাচ্চু বুরুংচি রেআ mácchu burungchi réá; "*the cow goes into the jungle*" or with equal propriety, mácchu burungoná *or* chiná réá.

Note The use of these affixes is governed also largely by euphony.

8. *Vocative case.*—Nouns of simple address or exclamation are said to be in the vocative case. They are designated by ও, *o*, or some word of exclamation going before, as, ও সালগিও দংগিপ্পা আফা, o Sálgio dangippá Aphá, "*oh, Father in Heaven.*"

Note. Very frequently the nasal ন, *n*, sound is added to the pronunciation of these case endings, making of খো, *kho*, খোন *khon;* চি, *chi*, চিন, *chin;* ও, *o*, ওন্, *on*, (long *o*) *&c.* This is both for the sake of emphasis and euphony.

The following table will show at a glance the different cases and their signs as used in Garo.

SINGULAR NUMBER.

Nom.	মান্দে	mánde	*a man.*
Obj.	মান্দেখো	mándékho	*a man.*
Inst.	মান্দেচি	mándéchi	*by a man.*
Dat.	মান্দেনা	mándéna	*to a man.*
Abl.	মান্দেওনি, ওনিখো	mándéoni or onikho	*from a man.*
Poss.	মান্দেনি	mándéni	*of a man.*
Loc.	মান্দে, ও, ওনা, চি	mándé o, oná or chi	*in or to a man.*
Voc.	ও মান্দে	o mándé	*oh man!*

PLURAL NUMBER.

Nom.	মান্দেরাং	mándéráng	*men*
Obj.	মান্দেরাংখো	mánderangkho	*men.*
Inst.	মান্দেরাংচি	mándéráńgchi	*by men.*
Dat.	মান্দেরাংনা	mándérángná	*to men.*
Abl.	মান্দেরাংওনি, ওনিখো	mándérang oni or onikho	*from men.*
Poss.	মান্দেরাংনি	mándérangni,	*of men.*
Loc.	মান্দেরাংও, ওনা, চি চিনা	mándérángo oná or chi chiná	*in or to men*
Voc.	ও মান্দেরাং	o mándéráng	*oh men!*

In the same way decline;

মেচিক্	méchik.	*a woman*

আচিক্	áchik	*Garo*
আব্রি	ábri	*mountain*
আমাক্	ámák	*monkey*
আচাক্	áchák	*dog*
মাচ্ছা	mácchá	*tiger*
মাচ্ছু	mácchu	*cow*
মেংগ	menga	*cat*
মাপিল	mápil.	*bear*
দোবিমা	dobimá	*cock*

CHAPTER III.

PRONOUNS.

In Garo are found personal, relative, interrogative, demonstrative and adjective pronouns.

Section first;—Personal Pronouns.

	Singular number.			Plural number.		
1	আংআ	Angá	*I*	চিংআ	Chingá	*We*
2	নাআ	Náá	*You*	নাশিমাং	Náshimáng	*You or ye*
3	উয়া	Uá	*He*	উয়ামাদাং	Uámádáng	*They.*

Note. The second and the third person plural forms are only the forms of the singular qualified by an adverb meaning number. For this reason the form of the plural varies according to the adverb that may be used. As,. instead of উয়ামাদাং uámádáng, উয়ামাং uámáng is often used;—মাং mang being an adverb equivalent to মাদাং madang. This again is varied with রাং ráng.

The following table will show the method of declining the pronouns.

SINGULAR NUMBER,—FIRST PERSON.

Nom.	আংআ	ángá	*I.*
Obj.	আংখো	ángkho	*me.*
Inst.	আংচি	ángchi	*by me.*
Dat.	আংনা	ángná	*to me.*
Abl.	আংওনি, ওনিখো	ángoni, onikho	*from me.*
Poss.	আংনি	ángni	*of me, mine.*
Loc.	আংও	ángo	*in me.*
Voc.	ও আংআ	O ángá	*O me.*

SECOND PERSON.

Nom.	নাআ	náá	*you*
Obj.	নাংখো	nángkho	*you*
Inst.	নাংচি	nángchi	*by you*
Dat.	নাংনা	nángná	*to you*
Abl.	নাংওনি, ওনিখো	nángoni, onikho	*from you*
Poss.	নাংনি	nángni	*of you, yours*
Loc.	নাংও	nángo	*in you*
Voc.	ও নাআ	O náá	*O you, thou.*

THIRD PERSON.

Nom.	উয়া	uá	*he*
Obj.	উয়াখো	uákho	*him*
Inst.	উয়াচি	uáchi	*by him*
Dat.	উয়ানা	uáná	*to him*
Abl.	উয়াওনি, ওনিখো	uáoni, onikho	*from him*
Poss.	উয়ানি	uáni	*of him or his*
Loc.	উয়াও	uáo	*in him.*
Voc.			

Note 1. In the pronoun of the first person the last syllable আ *áh* is dropped in all the cases except the nominative; it giving place to the case affix.

2. In the pronoun of the second person in all the cases except the nominative the last syllable is dropped and in its place "ং" *ng, anuswar*, is taken before the case affix.

3. In the third person the last syllable, আ "*áh*" is often dropped in conversation. As, for উয়াখো, uá-kho, say উখো *ukho &c.*

PLURAL NUMBER,—FIRST PERSON.

Nom.	চিংআ	chingá	*we*
Obj.	চিংখো	chingkho	*us*
Inst.	চিংচি	chingchi	*by us*
Dat.	চিংনা	chingná	*to us*
Abl.	চিংওনি-ওনিখো	chingoni, onikho	*from us*
Poss.	চিংনি	chingni	*ours, of us*
Loc.	চিংও	chingo	*in us.*

SECOND PERSON.

Nom.	নাসিমাং	náshimáng	*you or ye*
Obj.	নাসিমাংখো	náshimángkho	*you or ye*
Inst.	নাসিমাংচি	náshimángchi	*by you*
Dat.	নাসিমাংনা	náshimángná	*to you*
Abl.	নাসিমাংওনি, ওনিখো	náshimángoni, or onikho	*from you*
Poss.	নাসিমাংনি	náshimángni	*of you, your*
Loc.	নাসিমাংও	náshimángo	*in you.*

THIRD PERSON.

Nom.	উয়ামাং	uámáng	*they*
Obj.	উয়ামাংখো	uámángkho	*them*

Inst	উয়ামাংচি	uámángchi	*by them*
Dat.	উয়ামাংনা	uámángná	*to them*
Abl.	উয়ামাংওনি, or ওনিখো	uámángoni, or onikho	*from them*
Poss.	উয়ামাংনি	uámángni	*of them, theirs*
Loc.	উয়ামাংও	uámángo	*in them.*

Note. In the first person plural, as in the first singular, in declension the plural syllable আ "*áh*" is dropped before the case affix. Instead of চিংআখো chingákho, say চিংখো chingkho *&c.*

Section Second;—Relative Pronouns.

In the Garo language the relative pronouns are;

	Singular,		Plural.	
Relative	জে, jé	*he who that which.*	জেরাং jéráng,	*they which &c.*

Corelative, উয়া uá *he, she, it.* উয়ামাং uámáng, *they.*

Note 1. These pronouns are declined in the same way as the personal pronouns.

Note 2. In use, contrary to the English method the relative is in the first member of the sentence; as জেখো নাআ নিক্খেন উয়াখো অকাম্বো jékho náá nikkhen uákho akámbo, "*he whom you will see, call him.*

জেরাং এবাগেন উয়ামাংখো আগান্বো jéráng ebágen, uámángkho áganbo "*they who will come, tell them,*" *&c.*

Section Third;—Interrogative Pronouns.

These are, for the

	SINGULAR,			PLURAL.
সা, সাওয়া	shá, sháoá	*who?*	সারাং	*who? what people?*
মায়,	mái	*what?*	মায়রাং	*what things?*

These are declined in the same way as the personal pronouns.

Section Fourth;—Demonstrative Pronouns.

These are for the

	SINGULAR,			PLURAL.	
ইয়া	iá	*this*	ইয়ারাং	iáráng	*these*
উয়া	uá	*that*	উয়ারাং	uáráng	*those.*

Declinable as the other pronouns.

Section Fifth;—Adjective Prounouns.

In Garo these are quite numerous, some of which are given below;—

গিপিন	gippin	*other*
সাওবা	sháobá	*some, one*
অন্থিসা	anthishá	*some*
বাংআ	bángá	*many*
সাকান্থি	shákánthi	*each*
বাসিক্সাক	báshikshak	*how many?*
ইন্দিতা	inditá	*so many*
সাক্সা	shákshá	*some one*
বাদিগিতা	bádigitá	*how many?*

ইন্দিগিতা	indigitá	*so many*
জেগিতা	jégitá	*as many*
ইন্দিতা	inditá	*so many*
আস্খি	áskhi	*such an one*
আরসারক	árshárak.	*another*
আরঅন্থিসা	áranthishá	*some more*
জেগিপিন	jégippin	*another one who.*

CHAPTER IV.

ADJECTIVES.

Section First;—Of Qualifying Adjectives.

Adjectives describe the quality or property of nouns as বিসা নাম্মা bisá námmá *a good boy;* নাম্মা námmá qualifies boy. মান্দে আন্সেংআ mándé ánsengá *a happy man.* Adjectives are often made intensive by adverbs as বিসা নাম্মেন নাম্মা besá námmen námmá *a very good boy:* নাম্মেন námmen is an adverb, *very.*

2. Adjectives as a rules *follow* the noun which they qualify, as মান্দে নিথোআ mánde nithoá "*a handsome man*" বলচুআ balchuá "*a high tree.*" *&c.* There are some exceptions to this rule however.

3. There is no agreement in gender in adjectives. Adjectives of the same form qualify nouns of either masculine, feminine or neuter gender, as, মান্দে নাম্মা mánde námmá, *a good man;* মেচিক নাম্মা méchik námmá, *a good woman;* বলনাম্মা balnámmá *a good tree.*

4. The comparison of nouns, is made by means of the word বাতে báté, (with the sense of *than*) com-

ing after the noun with which comparison is made and the word বাতা *bátá* or বেয়া *béá*, joined to or compounded with the qualifying adjective, thus, ইয়া খানচানা বাতে উয়া খানচা নাম্বাতা or নাম্বেয়া, "iá kháncháná báté, uá khánchá nánbátá," or "nambéa," *that cloth is better than this.* Literally, *than this cloth, that cloth is good.*

Note. বাতে báté, *from* or *than* always takes the dative case, না *ná* before it. As, খানচা khánchá, খান্চানা বাতে khánchána báté.

5. Degrees of comparison are expressed in what to our ears is a very clumsy method. It is something as follows ইয়া আচাক্ চন্না, iá áchák channá, *this dog is small;* ইয়া আচাক্না বাতে, উয়া আচাক্ চন্বাতা iá áchákná báté, uá áchák chanbátá, *that dog is smaller than this;* ইয়া আচাক মাংগিথামনি গিসেপো, ইয়া আচাক চনবাতা iá áchák mángithámni gishepo, iá áchák chanbátá, *among these three dogs, this dog is little,* i. e. *is least of all the three.* In the same way the highest degree of comparison of all may be made by using some adverb meaning *all,* or *the whole* before the noun with which comparison is made, as বল দ্রাংনা বাতে ইয়া বল চুবাতা bal drángná báté iá bal chubátá, *this tree is the tallest of all trees.* Literally, *than all trees, this tree is very tall.*

6. A peculiarity of adjectives in this language is their capability of being conjugated as verbs, in which case they serve the purpose of both the adjective and auxillary verb thus উয়া বিসা নাম্মা uá bisá

námmá, *that boy is good,* and উয়া বিসা নাম্‌গেন্ uá bisá námgen, *that boy will be,* or *become good,* (will improve.) Here the idea of future improvement is expressed by the verbal sign of the future tense .(গেন, gen) joined to the first syllable of the adjective, meaning *good* i. e. নাম্মা námmá. In the conjugation, the last part of the adjective gives place to the verbal inflection. In the same way ইয়া বিথে দালেংআ iá bithé dálénga, *this fruit is becoming large.* In this case, দাল্লা, *dállá* expresses the quality of size (largeness) and এংআ *éngá*, that of progression in size.

This form is of frequent occurrence, and is used in respect of distance, as increasing or diminishing of sickness, as growing worse or better *&c. &c.*

Section Second;—Of Numeral Adjectives.

The Garo language has its system of notation with its numbers running up to—. For these numbers however it has previously had no cypher or other symbols. The figures used in the Bengali language have been adopted to represent the words of notation existing in the Garo. The system will be found very simple.

1	সা	shá	one
2	গ্নি	gni	two
3	গিথাম	githám	three
4	ব্রি	bri	four
5	বংআ	bangá	five
6	দক্	dak	six

7	স্নি	sni	seven
8	চেত	chet	eight
9	স্খু	skhu	nine
10	চিখুং	chikhung	ten
11	চিসা	chisá	eleven
12	চিগ্নি	chigni	twelve
13	চিগিথাম	chigithám	thirteen
14	চিব্রি	chibri	fourteen
15	চিবংআ	chibangá	fifteen
16	চিদক্	chidak	sixteen
17	চিস্নি	chisni	seventeen
18	চিচেত	chichet	eighteen
19	চিস্খু	chiskhu	nineteen
20	খল্‌গ্রিক্	khalgrik	twenty
21	খল্‌গ্রিক্ সা	khalgrikshá	twenty-one
22	খল্‌গ্রিক্ গ্নি	khalgrik gni	twenty-two
23	খল্‌গ্রিক্ গিথাম	khalgrik githám	twenty-three
24	খলগ্রিক্ ব্রি	khalgrik bri	twenty-four
25	খল্‌গ্রিক্ বংআ	khalgrik bangá	twenty-five
26	খল্‌গ্রিক্ দক্	khalgrik dak	twenty-six
27	খল্‌গ্রিক্ স্নি	khalgrik sni	twenty-seven
28	খল্‌গ্রিক্ চেত	khalgrik chet	twenty-eight
29	খল্‌গ্রিক্ স্খু	kholgrik skhu	twenty-nine
30	খলাত্‌চি	khalátchi	thirty
31	খলাত্‌চি সা	khalátchi shá	thirty-one
32	খলাতচি গ্নি	khalátchi gni	thirty-two
33	খলাত্‌চি গিথাম্	khalátchi githám	thirty-three
34	খলাত্‌চি ব্রি	kalátchi bri	thirty-four

35	খলাত্চি বংআ	khalátchi bangá	thirty-five
36	খলাত্চি দক্	khalátchi dak	thirty-six
37	খলাত্চি স্নি	khalátchi sni	thirty-seven
38	খলাত্চি চেত্	khalátchi chet	thirty-eight
39	খলাত্চি স্খু	khalátchi skhu	thirty-nine
40	সত্ব্র	shatbri	forty
41	সত্ব্র সা	shatbri shá	forty-one
42	সত্ব্র গ্নি	shatbri gni	forty-two
43	সত্ব্র গিথাম	shatbri githám	forty-three
44	সত্ব্র ব্রি	shatbri bri	forty-four
45	সত্ব্র বংআ	shatbri bangá	forty-five
46	সত্ব্র দক্	shatbri dak	forty-six
47	সত্ব্র স্নি	shatbri sni	forty-seven
48	সত্ব্র চেত	shatbri chet	forty-eight
49	সত্ব্র স্খু	shatbri skhu	forty-nine
50	সত্বংআ	shatbangá	fifty
51	সত্বংআ সা	shatbangá shá	fifty-one
52	সত্বংআ গ্নি	shatbangá gni	fifty-two
53	সত্বংআ গিথাম	shatbangá githám	fifty-three
54	সত্বংআ ব্রি	shatbangá bri	fifty-four
55	সত্বংআ বংআ	shatbangá bangá	fifty-five
56	সত্বংআ দক্	shatbangá dak	fifty-six
57	সত্বংআ স্নি	shatbangá sni	fifty-seven
58	সত্বংআ চেত	shatbangá chet	fifty-eight
59	সত্বংআ স্খু	shatbangá skhu	fifty-nine
60	সত্দক্	shatdak	sixty
61	সত্দক্ সা	shatdak shá	sixty-one
62	সত্দক্ গ্নি	shatdak gni	sixty-two
63	সত্দক্ গিথাম	shatdak githám	sixty-three

64	সতদক্ ব্রি	shatdak bri	sixty-four
65	সত্দক্ বংআ	shatdak bangá	sixty-five
66	সত্দক্ দক্	shatdak dak	sixty-six
67	সত্দক্ স্নি	shatdak sni	sixty-seven
68	সত্দক চেত	shatdak chet	sixty-eight
69	সত্দক্ স্খু	shatdak skhu	sixty-nine
70	সত্স্নি	shatsni	seventy
71	সত্স্নি সা	shatsni shá	seventy-one
72	সত্স্নি গ্নি	shatsni gni	seventy-two
73	সত্স্নি গিথাম	shatsni githám	seventy-three
74	সত্স্নি ব্রি	shatsni bri	seventy-four
75	সত্স্নি বংআ	shatsni bangá	seventy-five
76	সত্স্নি দক্	shatsni dak	seventy-six
77	সত্স্নি স্নি	shatsni sni	seventy-seven
78	সত্স্নি চেত	shatsni chet	seventy-eight
79	সত্স্নি স্খু	shatsni skhu	seventy-nine
80	সত্চেত	shatchet	eighty
81	সত্চেতসা	shatchet sha	eighty-one
82	সত্চেত গ্নি	shatchet gni	eighty-two
83	সত্চেত গিথাম	shatchet githám	eighty-three
84	সত্চেত ব্রি	shatchet bri	eighty-four
85	সত্চেত বংআ	shatchet bangá	eighty-five
86	সত্চেত দক্	shatchet dak	eighty-six
87	সত্চেত স্নি	shatchet sni	eighty-seven
88	সত্চেত চেত	shatchet chet	eighty-eight
89	সত্চেত স্খু	shatchet skhu	eighty-ninety
90	সত্স্খু	shatskhu	ninety
91	সত্স্খু সা	shatskhu sha	ninety-one
92	সত্স্খু গ্নি	shatskhu gni	ninety-two

93	সত্স্খু গিথাম	shatskhu githám	ninty-three
94	সত্স্খু ব্রি	shatskhu bri	ninty-four
95	সত্স্খু বংআ	shatskhu bangá	ninety-five
96	সত্স্খু দক	shatskhu dak	ninty-five
97	সত্স্খু স্নি	shatskhu sni	ninty-seven
98	সত্স্খু চেত	shatskhu chet	ninety-eight
99	সত্স্খু স্খু	shatskhu skhu	ninety-nine
100	রিত্ছাসা	ritccháshá	one-hundred
200	রিচ্ছাগ্নি	ritcchagni	two-hundred
1000	হাজাল সা	házál shá	one-thousand
10000	হাজালচিখুং	házálchikung	ten-thousand

CHAPTER V.

OF VERBS.

The verb is the most complicated and difficult part of the Garo language.

Like all verbs it has voices, moods and tenses, persons and participles. Of voices it may be said to have properly two, active and passive though the passive form is sometimes used with a causal sense.

There are five moods, the indicative, the subjunctive, the potential, the imperative and the infinitive.

The subjunctive and potential however are not conjugated regularly, but with the help of other words.

There are seven tenses, sometimes used, the present, the present progressive, the simple past, the simple past progressive, the remote or indefinite past and its progressive, and the future.

Section First.—Regular Verb, Active Voice.

Every regular verb is conjugated from a root or stem which has a substantive sense, and is properly called a verbal noun. The different tenses (or times) of the action designated by the substantive word are indicated by affixes. Thus দক্ dak, root, *strike* or "*a striking,*" and দকা daká, *I strike.* Here the affix আ áh, indicates that the striking is done in present time, দকেংআ dakéngá, *I am striking.* Here এংআ "*engá*" shows the *progressive* nature of the action *&c.*

Observe.—In Garo the nominative case alone designates the person and number of the verb. The affixes are the same for all persons and both numbers.

The following table will exhibit the different forms of the verb in its various tenses *&c.*

Conjugation of the regular verb দক্না dakná, *to strike.*

1. Indicative Mood.—*Present Tense.*

	Singular.			Plural.			
1	আংআ	ángá	I,	চিংআ	chingá	we	দকা daká *strike or strikes.*
2	নাআ	náá	you,	নাসিমাং	násimáng	ye	
3	উয়া	uá	he,	উয়ামাদাং	uámadáng	they	

Present Progressive Tense.

1 Sing.
2 or
3 Plu. } দকেংআ dakengá, *am, are, is striking.*

Simple Past Tense.

1 Sing.
2 or
3 Plu. } দকাহা বা দক্জক্ dakáhá or dakjak, *struck, or have struck.*

Indefinite or Remote Past Tense.

1 Sing. }
2 or } দকাহাচিম dakáháchim, *had struck.*
3 Plu. }

Progressive Past Tense.

1 Sing. }
2 or } দকেংআহাচিম dakéngáháchim, *was striking.*
3 Plu. }

Future Tense.

1 Sing. }
2 or } দক্গেন বা খেন, dakgen or khen, *shall or will strike.*
3 Plu. }

2. Imperative Mood.

2 Pers. দক্বো dakbo *you or ye strike.*

3 Pers. দকচিনা বা দক্চং dakchiná or chang, *let him or them strike.*

3. Infinitive Mood.

দকনা dakná, *to strike.*

4. Participles.

Present, দকোদে, dakode, *striking, (with hypothetical sense.)*

" দকোয়া dakoá, *striking (having reference to time.)*

Past or perfect, দকে বা দকেমু বা দকেন্বা daké, émú or énbá, *having struck.*

5. Subjunctive or Conditional Mood.

This mood has properly but two tenses.

Future tense.—This is expressed by means of the present participle ওদে ode and the future tenses, thus (আংআ ángá উয়াখো uákho নিকোদে nikode, উয়ানা uạná খাসাগেন káságen) "*I seeing him will love him,*" or "*if I see him, I will love him.*

Past Tense.—This tense of the subjunctive is expressed by means of the signs of the future and the indefinite past tenses being joined to both members of the clause. Thus, আংআ উয়াখো নিক্‌গেন্‌চিম ইন্দিদে উয়ানা আংআ খাসাগেনচিম **ángá** uákho nikgenchim endidé uáná ángá káságenchim, *Had I seen him (then) I would have loved him.*

Note. This form of the subjunctive always implies that the reverse of the supposition is true, as above, *not seeing him I did not love him.*

6. Potential Mood.

This mood is only expressed with the help of other words. The two auxillaries most frequently used to express potentiality are মান্না, **mánná** *to get*, and আঃম্ম **ámmá** *to be able*, placed after the verb in the infinitive mood. Thus, আংআ ইয়া খামখো খানা আঃম্মা Angá eá kámkho khánά ámmá, *I can do*, (or am able to do) *this work.*

Note. This mood may be used in any of the tenses of the regular verb by conjugating the auxillary, or potential verb.

Section Second.—Passive and Causal Verbs.

These are classed together because they are exactly alike in conjugation, both the passive and causal senses being indicated by inserting the syllable, আত "*át*" between the verbal stem and the ordinary tense affix. The passive is distinguished from the causal by having the objective case before it instead of a nominative.

Conjugation of the passive and causal verb,

দক্না dakná, *to strike.*

INDICATIVE MOOD.—*Present Tense.*

1 আংখো বা আংআ, ángkho, or ángá
2 নাংখো বা নাআ, nángkho, or náá
3 উয়াখো বা উয়া, uákho, or uá
} দকাতা, dakátá, *struck or cause to strike.*

Present Progressive.

1 SING. 2 or 3 PLU. } দকাতেংআ dakátengá, *being struck or causing to strike.*

Simple Past.

1 SING. 2 or 3 PLU. } দকাতাহা, dakátáhá, *was struck,* or *caused to strike.*

Indefinite or *Remote Past.*

1 SING. 2 or 3 PLU. } দকতাহাচিম dakatáháchim, *have or had been struck,* or *had caused to strike.*

Indefinite Past Progressive.

1 SING. 2 or 3 PLU. } দকাতেংআহাছিম, dakáténgáháchim, *was being struck or was causing to strike.*

Future Tense.

1 SING. 2 or 3 PLU. } দকাত্গেন বা খেন dakatgen, or khen *will be struck or will cause to strike.*

IMPERATIVE MOOD.

2. দকাত্বো dakátbo, *be struck or cause to strike.*

3. দকাত্চিনা বা চং dakátchená or chang, *let him be struck or let him cause to strike.*

INFINITIVE MOOD.

দকাত্না *to be struck, or to cause to strike.*

Participles.

Present—দকাত্তোমে, *being struck; or causing to strike.*

Past—দকাতে বা মুং, এন্বা, *having been struck, or caused to strike.*

Section Third.—Negative Verbs.

The formation of the negative verb is so peculiar and differs to such an extent from the regular conjugation that it is thought best to give it a section and table to itself.

Conjugation of the verb, দক্না dakná *to strike,* in its negative form.

Indicative Mood.—*Present Tense.*

1 Sing. 2 or 3 Plu.	দক্জা dakjá, *strike, or strikes not, or does not strike.*

Present Progressive.

1 Sing. 2 or 3 Plu.	দক্জাএংআ, dakjáéngá *am, are, or is not striking.*

Simple Past.

1 Sing. 2 or 3 Plu.	দক্জাজক্ বা খুজা, dakjájak or dakkhujá, *did not strike, or have not struck.*

Indefinite or Remote Past.

1 Sing. 2 or 3 Plu.	দক্জাহাচিম / দক্খুজাচিম	dakjáháchim / dakkhujáchim	*had not struck.*

Indefinite Past Progressive.

1 Sing. 2 or 3 Plu.	দক্জাএংআচিম dakjáéngáchim, *uas not, have not been, or had not been, striking.*

Future Tense.

1 SING. 2 or 3 PLU.	দক্জাওয়া dakjáoá *will not strike.*

IMPERATIVE MOOD.

2	দক্নাবে বা দাদক, daknábé or dádak, *do not strike.*
3	দক্জাচিম, জাচং dakjáchim, or jáchang, *let him not strike.*

PARTICIPLES.

Present—দক্জাওদে dakjáode *not striking, (with hypothetical sense.)*

Present—দক্জাওয়া, dakjáoá, *not striking, (with reference to time.)*

Past—দক্গিজা, জাএমু, বা জাএনবা, dakgijá, jáému, or jáenba, *not having struck.*

Note. The subjunctive and potential moods are conjugated in the same way, i. e. by inserting the negative adverb জা বা খুজা *ja* or *khujá* after the stem or root of the verb. In the potential mood it is inserted in the auxilliary or potential verb.

Section Fourth.—Of Compound Verbs.

Verbs of a compound form are in constant use in Garo and a knowledge of them is very essential to any progress in the use of the language.

Verbs are compounded with almost all the different parts of speech, as nouns, adjectives, other verbs, adverbs, prepositions and conjunctions.

1. *With Nouns.*—This most usually occurs when some substantive is united to the verb খাআ kháá *to do, to perform* as, for, *Iam working,* say, আংআ খামখায়েংআ ángá khámkháengá. খামখায়েংআ khámkháengá expresses the idea of *being engaged in work,* or *doing business.*

2. *With Adjectives.*—Some of the cases in which this form occurs have already been given. See Adjec. Sec. first, Note 6. In this combination, the verbal affix always joins to the first syllable of the adjective word and in this way may be conjugated through all the moods and tenses as, আংনি বেয়েনি সা নাম্মেংআ ángni béyéni shá námmengá, *my health is improving,* lit, *the sickness of my body is becoming good.* Here নাম্মা námmá, is the adjective *well, good.* Its final syllable being dropped, its first is attached to the affix of the progressive present tense of the verb আংআ ángá, to *become.* In this way the rather dubious idea of *sickness* improving or becoming good is literally given, while the contrary sense of sickness departing and health returning is meant.

Under this rule a double compound is very common, as, when the quality of an object is set forth by the verb *as acting,* and as acting in a particular manner by another verb compounded with the first, thus বলচুবায়েংআ bal-chu-báengá, *the tree is growing,* lit, *the tree is becoming high, very* literally, the tree is *highing.* In this case the adjective is compounded with two verbs ইবাআ ibáá *to come,* and আংআ ángá, *to become,* while the adjective was চুআ chuá, *high.*

In the same way বিসা দাল্‌বায়েংআ bishá dálbáengá, *the child is growing*, from দাল্লা dállá *large*, ইবআ ibaá, *to come*, and এংআ éngá present progressive tense of আংআ ángá, *to become*.

2 Verbs are also compounded with adjectives expressive of number, of and in such a way as to form a sort of agreement of the verb with its case both nominative and objective, thus নাআ ইবাবো náá ibábo, *you come*, but নাসিমাং ইবাথক্‌বো náshimáng ibáthakbo *you all come*, থক্‌ thak, expresses *number* and is always inserted between the verbal stem and its affix.

Instead of থক্‌ thak, চিম chim is sometimes used in the same way, as দারাংআন্‌ রেয়াংচিমা dárángán réang-chimá *all* or *many come*.

Note.—It will frequently be seen that even when the adjective expressive of plurality of number is compounded, as above, with the verb, another adjective similarly expressing plurality precedes the verb, as, রাজা দারাং মান্দেরাংখো দকে গাল্‌থকাহা rájá dáráng mánde rángkho daké gálthakáhá, *the king killed all the men*.

3. With other Verbs.—This construction is constantly met with in the Garo. The following examples will give an idea of the general principle, viz উখো আংআ রিম্‌বাগেন, ukho ángá rimbágen, *I will bring him*. Here the two verbs রিম্মা rimmá, *to seize* and ইবাআ ibáá *to come* are combined and put in the future tense by the affix গেন gen. রুআখো রাবাবো ruákho rábábo *bring the axe*, রাআ ráá *to take* and, as above ইবাআ are compounded and used in the imperative mood.

Note 1. রিম্মা rimmá *to sieze* is used only in respect of animate things and রাআ ráá *to take* of inanimate.

Note 2. These words রিম্মা rimmá, and রাআ ráá are also compounded with রেঙ্গাংআ réángá *to go*, to express the idea of taking away as, সাহেব উয়া বিসাখো রিমাংজক্ sáheb uá bishákho rimmángjak, *saheb took that boy away.* নাআ খিতাপখো রাআংবো, náá khitápkho ráángbo, *you take the book away.*

Note. 3. A double compound is used when the idea of returning or bringing back, or taking away again is desired to be expressed, as, আংআ নাংখোন রম্বিাফিল্গেন ángá nángkhon rimbáphilgen, *I will bring you back.* Here the three verbs রিম্মা rimmá, *to sieze,* ইবাআ ibáá, *to come* and ফিল্লা phillá, *to turn, to turn about* are compounded in to the one রিম্বাফিল্লা rimbáphillá, used in this case in the future tense. In the same way, রাআংফিল্বো ráángphilbo, *take it back again or return it.*

4. With Adverbs.—These are chiefly seen in the case of adverbs of time, as, আগান্মানো ágánmáno *after speaking,* Here আগান্না ágánná, *to speak* is compounded with জামানো jámáno, *afterwards,* or *in the time after.* The final syllable of the verb and the first of the adverb are eliminated. In the same way রেয়াংমিতিংও reyángmitingo, *in the time of going,* from রেয়াংআ reyángá *going,* and মিতিংও mitingo *at the time of,* আংআ ইবামিতিংও মাৎছা মাংসাখো নিকাহা, ángá ibámitingo mátchá mángshákho nikáhá, *as I was coming,* or *in the time of coming I saw one tiger.*

5. Verbs also receive into their body as a component part, words which in the English usually rank as prepositions thus, বিসারাং খাল্‌গ্রিকেংআ, bisháráng khálgrikengá, *the children are playing together.* Here খাল্লা khállá, *to play,* takes in গ্রিক্ grik, *with, together.* মান্দেরাং দকগ্রিকা, mándéráng dakgriká, *the men fight.* Another form, আগানা ágáná, *to speak*, and আগান্থায়া ágántháiá, *to speak again*, থায়া tháiá, *again.* Some of these are properly derivative verbs, as দকা daká, *to strike*, and দক্গ্রিকা dakgriká, *to strike together*, i. e. *to fight.* আগানা ágáná, *to speak*, and আগান্থায়া ágántháiá, *to speak again i. e. to repeat.*

6 Verbs often form substantives by being joined to the word গিপ্পা, gippá *person, individual*, as দাক্কা dákká, *to do or a doing*, and দাক্গিপ্পা dákgippá *a doer, one who does.* আগানা, ágáná, *to speak*, and আগানগিপ্পা ágángippá, *a speaker.* রেবাআ rebáá, *to come*, and রেবাগিপ্পা rébágippá *a comer.* সক্বাআ sahkbáá, *to arrive*, and সক্বাগিপ্পা, shakbágippá, *one who arrives*, and by derivation *a stranger* or *guest.*

Section Fifth.—General Remarks on the Verb.

It would be useless to attempt to generalize from an unwritten language spoken by a totally uncultured people a set of rules for the use of the verb that would admit of rigid application in all cases; yet it is hoped that the following hints will afford a guide to a *beginning* in the use of this part of the Garo language,—a beginning which can be carried on to perfection only by long practice.

1. *Irregular Verbs.*—A few verbs of this class are in constant use. That most usually heard is গ্নাং or গিনাং, gnáng, *to be.* It is used only in the present and indefinite past tenses, as আচক্ নকো গ্নাং, áchak nako gnáng, *the dog is in the house.* বিসা রামাও গ্নাং, bishá rámáo gnáng, *the child is in the road.* আংআ উয়া সংও গ্নাংচিম, Angá uá shango gnángchim, *I was in that village.* নাআ বুরুংও গ্নাংচিম, náá burungo gnángchim, *you were in the jungle.* গ্রি, gri, *not being,* is a negative verb of the same kind as the foregoing, as, আংও থাংখা গংসাবা গ্রি, Ango thángkhá gangshábá gri, *I have no money,* litrally *in me one rupee even is not,* গ্রি gri expresses the negative idea, *is not.* This meaning is otherwise expressed by দংজা dangjá, the negative form of the verb, *to remain.* আআরে áárė, may also be classed as an irregular verb used chiefly in giving a negative answer to questions, as, নাংনি সা গ্নাংমা? আআরে nángni shá gnángmá? aáré. *Are you ill?* (lit, *have you sickness*) answer, *I have not,* or *it* (sickness) *is not.*

2. *Necessity and Obligation,* are always expressed by means of নাংআ nángá, used with a verb in the infinitive mood, as নাআ ইয়া খাম্খো খানা নাংআ, náá iá khámkho kháná nángá, *you must do this work.* আংআ উনোনা রেয়াংনা নাংগেন্, Angá unoná reángná nánggen, *I will have to go there.* In the same way দারাংআন্ ইসল্না খাসানা নাংআ, dárángán Ishálná kháshaná nángá, *all ought to love God.* মাআ ফানি খাথাখো রাঃনা নাংআ máá pháni khátákho raána nángá, *it is right* or *proper to obey mother and father,* lit, *one* (nom. understood) *ought to receive the words of mother and father.*

Note. This verb নাংআ, nángá, meaning originally *to apply, to join to,* may be conjugated through all the tenses of the regular verb.

3. The rules for the use of the voices and moods are the same as they would be in any language. The peculiarities of the formation of the potential and subjunctive moods have already been explained in the sections relating to them.

4. The use of the tenses is more uncertain. The *Present Tense,* is used in general statements and without reference to time, or expresses action as occurring in defined present time as আংআ রেবারা, Angá rebárá, *I go,* i. e. *I go,* but without stating *when.* আংআ দাও রেবারা, Angá dáo rebárá, *I now go.* But it will be observed that the form of the present tense is in sustained conversation and especially in narrative used to express action that occurred in past time.

5. *Present Progressive or Definite Tense.*—This tense is expressive of continued action in present time. Its sign is invariably এং éng, and is never used in any other form. খামাল্ খ্রিতেংআ, khámál khritengá, *the priest in sacrificing* i. e. the work is even new going on, and is not yet completed.

6. The *Simple Past or Imperfect,*—is used in describing an action just now done or in the immediately past, as আংআ মাচ্ছা মাংসা নিক্জক, ángá mácchá mángshá nikjak, *I saw a tiger.* উয়া মেরংখো চাআহা, uá mérangkho chááhạ, *he ate rice, or has eaten rice.* There is no appreciable differcnce in the use of the

two affixes জক্ jak and আহা áhá. They may be used interchangeably. The latter is most generally used in narrative.

7. *Remote or Indefinite Past.*—This tense is supposed to carry the hearer back to some point of time antecedent to some other subsequently mentioned time; or expresses action that occurred long since, as, আংআ সাহেবনি রেআংনা স্খাং খলিখাতাওনা রেআংআচিম, ángá sáhebni réángná skháng kholikhátáoná réángáchim, *before the sahib went away I visited Calcutta,* or *had gone to Calcutta.* Sometimes in expressing the remote past, the full form of the verb is not used, as in the example above given, where the syllable আ, "*áh*" is dropped before "চিম" "chim," which is really the sign of the *remote* past.

8. *The Past Progressive.*—is expressed in the same way as the present progressive, simply adding the sign of the "past immediate," or remote, and signifies that the action was going on, as, উআ ইবাএংআচিম uá ibáyengáchim, *he was coming.*

9. *Future Tense.*—The future simply declares that an action will take place hereafter. It is expressed in different localities in different ways, and in fact in the same localities variously, as, আংআ তুরাওনা রেনিম বা রেনাসা বা রেনাকা বা রেখেন বা রেগেম, ángá turáoná rénim or rénáshá or rénáká or rékhen or régém, either of which means that, "*I will go to Tura.*"

10. *Imperative Mood.*—The imperative is used chiefly in commanding, occasionally in entreaty. There

is no exclusive form for the first person. This is expressed by means of the infinitive mood and the imperative form, second person, of the verb *to give*, which in such cases has the sense of "allow" or "permit." Thus, আংনা নিনা অন্‌বো, ángná niná anbo, *allow me to see* or *give me to see.*

The second person imperative is used in cases of command. Its form has already been shown in the paradigm of verbs. The third person is used in entreaty, thus, হে সাল্‌গিও দংগিপ্পা আফা নাংনি নামনিকা চুসক্‌চিনা, Hé shálgio dangippá Aphá, nángni námniká chushakchiná, "*O Father which art in heaven thy will be done*" or *fulfilled.*

11. *Infinitive Mood.*—This is used to express the sense of the verb indefinitely as, আংআ ইয়া খামখো খানা মাংসংআ, ángá iá khámkho khánâ mángshangá; *I am prepared to do this work.* This is used also to express intention, as আংআ নিনা রেগেন্, ángá niná régen, *I will go to see* i. e. *for the purpose of*, or *with the intention of seeing*, I will go.

12. *Participles.*—The participles refer to present or future time, and to past. The present participle ওদে *odé*, is used chiefly in a conjunctive sense, and where "if" in English would be used, as আংআ উয়াখো নিকোদে আগান্‌গেন, "ángá uákho nikode ágángen," "*I seeing him will tell him.*" In such a sentence when emphasis is expressed the last syllable of the participle, (দে, *dé*) is dropped and the emphatic particle "বা" "*bá,*" substituted, as, নাআ উয়াখো নিকোবা আগান্-

বো, náá uákho nikobá ágánbo, "*if you see him tell him,*" i e as certainly as you see him tell him.

The past or perfect participle expresses the idea of one action having been performed, another followed in connection with it, as উআ আংখো নিকেন্‌বা অকাম্‌জক, uá ángkho nikenbá akámjak "*he having seen me called me.*"

13. *Substantive Verbs.*—Verbs are often used in a substantive sense, i. e. the action of the verb is construed as a definite object and as such is declined in the same way as nouns, as আংআ নাংনি আগানাখো খ্নাহা, ángá nángni áginákho knáhá, "*I heard your speaking.*" Here আগানা, ágáná, is properly the verb, *to speak* but is used as a noun in the objective case. আংআ রেআংও মান্দে বাংআখো নিকাহা anga reángo mánde bángákho nikáhá, *In going*, or *while going I saw many people.* রেআংআ, reángá, is the verb, *to go* but here used as a noun and put in the locative case, by the sign ও, *o*, literally, *in the going, I saw &c.* This substantive use of the verb is very common.

14. *Substantives formed from Verbs.*—This is done by joining the word গিপ্পা gippá, *person* to the verb, as, আগানা ágáná, *to speak,* and আগান্‌গিপা ágángippá *a speaker* রেয়াংআ reángá, *to go*, and রেগিপ্পা বা রেয়াংগিপ্পা, regippá or réánggippá *a goer;* দংআ dangá, *to remain* and দংগিপ্পা danggippá, *one who, or that which remains.* This rule is most constantly seen in Garo.

CHAPTER VI.

ADVERBS, PREPOSITIONS, CONJUNCTIONS AND INTERJECTIONS.

Section first.—Of Adverbs.

In the Garo language are found adverbs of time, of place, and of quality or manner.

1. Of Time.

Those of time are chiefly as follows;

দাআল, দাসাল,	dáál dáshál	} *to-day.*
মেজাল, মেজাসাল,	mejhál mejháshál	} *yesterday.*
খ্নাপ	khnápo	*to-morrow.*
দা বা দাও,	dá or dáo	*now, at this time.*
বাসাক	báshák	*when?*
জেন্সাল	jenshál	*when, at such a time which.*
উন্সাল	unshál	*then, at that time.*
মামুংসাল	mámungshál	*at any time.*
সালান্থি	shálánthi	*daily, every day.*
জ্রিংজ্রিং বা জ্রিংজ্রত্,	jringjring or jringjrot	*always.*
জামান বা জামানো,	jámán or jámáno.	*afterwards.*

ফ্রিংও,	phringo	*in the morning.*
সৎনি,	shatni	*day before yesterday.*
স্খাংও,	skhángo	*before, first in time.*
ওয়ালো,	ouálo	*in the night.*
আৎথানো	átthána	*in the evening.*
জেনাখিংখিং,	jenákhingkhing	*as long as.*
উনাখিংখিং,	unákhingkhing	*so long.*

Many adverbs of time are formed by adding আল, "ál" and সাল, shál meaning *day* or *time* to other words, as দাআল dáál, *to-day.* দা dá, means literally *now* and joined to আল ál, or সাল shál, we get *now day,* or *this day.* In the same way উন্সাল unshál a contraction from উয়ানি সাল uánishál, lit. *time of that,* comes to mean "*then*" &c.

2. *Of Place.*

ইয়ানো	iáno	*here.*
উয়ানো	uáno	*there.*
বানো বা বাও?	báno or báo	*where?*
বাওনি?	báoni	*whence, from where?*
জেও	jeo	*that place in which.*
ফ্লাক্চিন্,	phlákchin	*evry where, all directions.*
নিংও	ningo	*within.*
আফালো	áphálo	*without.*
স্খাংও	skhángo	*before, in front.*
মিখাংও	mikhángo	*near to, before.*
জামানো	jámáno	*behind.*

খোসাকো	khosháko	*above.*
জাফাংও	jáphángo	*below.*
চেল্লাও	chélláo	*far, distant.*

It will be seen that many adverbs of *place* are formed by means of the word signifying locality joined to the relative pronouns *this, that &c.*

In such cases these might properly be called "pronominal adverbs.

3. *Of Quality or Manner.*

নাম্মেন,	námmen,	*well, finely, in good manner.*
ইয়াগিত্তা	éágittá	*in this way.*
উয়াগিত্তা	uágittá	*in that way.*
মাএদাকে	máédáké	*in what way? how?*
অন্থিসা	anthishá,	*some, a few.*
বাংআ	bángá	*many, much.*
খাসিন্ খাসিন্	kháshin kháshin.	*by degrees, successively, slowly.*
নাম্মেদাকে	námedáké	*in good manner, well done.*
বেবেদাকে	bébédáké	*truly, truthfully.*
বাক্বাক্দাকে	bákbákdáké	*quickly, rapidly.*
নাংআ,	nángá,	*necessarily consequently.*
ইন্দিনারি	indinári	*causelessly.*
দংআরি	dangári	*vainly.*
দিংথাং	dingtháng	*differently.*
থল্লে	thallé	*falsely.*
ইন্দাকে	éndáké	*this way, thus.*

উন্দাকে	undáké	*that way.*
জেদাকে	jédáké	*that way which.*
মায়াদাকে	máédáké	*in what way.*

Many adverbs of manner are formed by joining the demonstrative and relative pronouns to the perfect participle of doing or performing, as ইন্দাকে indaké, *in this manner.* The first syllable ইন্ is a contract of ইয়ানি iáni, *of this,* while the last syllable দাকে dáké, is the perfect participle of the verb দাকা *to do* or *a doing.* So with উন্দাকে, জেদাকে, মায়খায়ে undáké, jédáké, máekháé, the latter from খাআ kháá *to do, to make &c.*

2. Adverbs are used in Garo to intensify adjectives, as বিসা নাম্মেন নাম্মা, bishá námmén námmá, *a very "good" boy.* নাম্মা, námmá, is the adjective "good" qualifying বিসা bishá, *boy,* and নাম্মেন námmén, is an adverb which may be rendered, "*very.*"

3, In the same manner one adverb is used to intensify another adverb, as ইয়া গুরে নাম্মেন গংরাকে দারিয়া, iá guré námmen gangráké dáriá, *this horse runs very swiftly.* In this sentence the adverb *swiftly* গংরাকে gangráké is composed of গং gng, *swift* and রাকে ráké, perfect participle of রাকা, *to do* or *perform,* নাম্মেন is the intensive adverb "*very.*" The sentence literally would read, "*this horse very fast having done, runs*"

4. Adverbs are sometimes compounded with verbs, or rather changed into verbs by the rules of conjugation, as ফ্রিংআহা, phringáhá, *morning came,* or *day*

broke. Here ফ্রিং phring, an adverb of time takes the affix of the verb of past tense.

Section Second.—Of Prepositons or Postpositions.

In Garo as in most of the languages of this country the words which correspond in meaning with "prepositions" in the English language are placed some before and some after the word to which they belong; hence some of then are properly *pre*-positions and some *post*-positions. The following list comprises those in most common use.

খো	kho	*upon, to.*
চি বা চিন্	chi or chin,	*with, in direction of, towards.*
না	ná	*to, on account of, by reason of.*
ওনি	oni	*from.*
ওনিখো	onikho	*away from.*
নি	ni	*of, denotes possession.*
আসোল	áshel	*on account of, reason for &c.*
বাক্সা	báksha	*with, in company of.*
ঝহাত্চি	jháhátchi,	*in the midst, among.*
আগ্রে	agré,	*before, in advance of, except.*
থাল্থাল্	thálthál	*from.*
খিংখিং	khingkhing	*to, up to, as far as.*
গিসেপো	gishepo,	*among, of, from.*
গিমিক্গিমাং দারাংমারাং	gimikgimáng dárángmáráng	} *all together.*
ফাল	phál	*instead of, in place of.*

আদাম ádám }
গিমিন gimin } *because of, for the sake of.*
দাম্বেংগিম্পেং dámbenggimpeng, *across, athwart.*
জাফাংও jáphángo *beneath, below.*

Note. As previously explained, some of these words are taken up by the verb and are conjugated with it as a compound part.

Of the prepositional words above given, গিমিন gimin, আসেল্ áshel, জাফাংও jáphángo গিসেপো, gishepo, জাত্চি, játchi, বাক্সা, bákshá, all govern the possessive case, as ইয়ানি গিমিন iáni gimin, *for this reason;* উনি আসেল্ uni áshel, *for that reason, on account of that;* বলনি জাফাংও, balni jáphángo, *at the bottom of the tree,* নাসিমাংনি গিসেপো, náshimángni gishepo, *among you, or from among you;* উয়ামাংনি জাত্চি, uámángni játchi, *in their midst, or in the midst of them,* আংনি বাক্সা ángni bákshá, *with me,* (this does not in all cases require the possessive case.) আগ্রে ágré, থাল্থাল্ thálthál, খিংখিং khingkhing &c., take the dative case, as উয়া মান্দেনা আগ্রে uá mándená ágré, *besides or except that man;* দাওনা থালথাল dáoná thálthál, *from this time (lit. from now.)* উনা খিংখিং uná khingkhing, *until then, that time.*

Section Third.—Of Conjunctions.

As in other languages conjunctions, in Garo, may be divided into two classes, Copulative and Disjunctive.

1. COPULATIVE.

আৰু	áru	*and.*
আৰোবা	árobá	*moreover, further.*
উনিগিমিন্	unigimin	*therefore consequently.*
ওদে	odé	*if.*
ইনদিদে	indidé	*then, in that case.*
আর	ár	*also, in addition, (seldom used.)*
বা	bá	*also, and.*
দাওবা	dáobá	*again.*
উনোসা	unoshá	*then,*
উয়ানো	uáno	*thereby.*
জেন্	jén	*in order that.*
জেনিগিমিন্	jénigimin,	*because, for the reason that.*
জেখায়	jékái	*as, so as.*
উয়াগিত্তা	uágittá	*so.*
ইন্দাকে	indáke	*so that.*
জে	jé	*that.*

2. DISJUNCTIVE.

ইন্দিবা	indibá	*but.*
বা	bá	*either, or.*
ওবা	obá	*although.*
ইন্দিবান্	indibán	*yet, notwithstanding.*
ইন্দিওবা	indiobá	*if not then, otherwise.*

Section Fourth.—Of Interjections.

The following words are used as interjections, or to express *surprise*.

হা, হায়,	há ! hái !	*to express sorrow.*
এ, এঃ	eh !	*to express pain.*

হিম,	him !	*expressive of admiration.*
ওঃ,	oh !	*of surprise.*
গসে,	gashe !	*of regret.*
রারারা,	rárárá !	*of remonstrance.*
আইওআই,	áieoái !	*of weariness.*
হাপ্বাপ্,	hápbáp !	*of regretful surprise.*
সাবাসি, নাম্মা,	sábáshi, námá !	*of praise.*
আত্চাও,	átcháo !	"*good*" "*well done.!*"
হম্মাংআই,	himmángáe !	*of disappointment.*
আআয়ও	ááio !	*of wonder, amazement.*

CHAPTER VII.

MISCELLANEOUS EXERCISES AND EXAMPLES.

Instead of devoting a chapter to the syntax of the language, I have added the following exercises and examples; believing that progress in its practical use may be better subserved in this way.

Section First.—Exercises in the Different Parts of Speech.

1. NOUNS.

Exercise.—1. In Number.

মান্দে রেবাআ
Mándé rebáá, A (or the) *man* comes.

আচাক দাআরিয়া
Achák dááriá, The *dog* runs.

মোত্‌চু ইনোনা রেবাএংআ
Mátchu inoná rébáéngá, The *cow* comes here.

মাত্‌চা বুরুংও দংআ
Mátchá burungo dangá, The *tiger* stays in the jungle.

ওয়াক আবাও গ্নাং
Owák ábáo gnáng, The *hog* is in the field.

মেচিক সাক্‌সা খাম খাএংআ
Mechik shákshá khám kháéngá, One *woman* is working.

বিসা খাদিংআ
Bishá khádingá, The *child* laughs.

নক্‌মা সাকগ্নি ইআংজক
Nakmá shákgni iángjak, The *Laskars* went.

মাপিল্‌ মাংব্রি রেআংআহা
Mápil mángbri réángáhá, Four *bears* went.

দো মাংবংআ দামসান বিলাংআ
Do mángbangá dámshán bilángá, Five *birds* are flying together.

বিসারাং খাল্‌গ্রিকা
Bisháráng khálgriká, The *children* play.

মেচিক বিসারাং খএংআ
Mechik bisháráng khaéngá, The *girls* are sewing.

মান্দেরাং চাথকাহা
Mánderáng cháthakáhá, The *men* have all eaten.

সাহেবরাং ইবাগেন
Sáhebráng ibágen, The *sahebs* will come.

দোরাং দাল্‌বাএংআ
Doráng dálbáengá, The *birds* are growing.

দারাংমান্দেরাং খাম খাথকগেন
Dárángmánderáng khám kháthakgen, All the *men* will work.

Exercise—2. In Gender.

নাংনি ফাখো অকামবো
Nángni phákho akámbo, Call your *father.*

ফান্থেরাংখো রিম্‌বাবো
Phánthérángkho rimbábo, Catch (or sieze) the *young men.*

বুদফানি গেয়েতাখো রাঃবো
Budepháni geyetákho ráabo, Respect the orders of the *aged.*

আংনি আদাথাং মামাথাং রেবায়েংআ
Angni ádátháng mámátháng rébáéngá, My brothers and uncles are coming.

মাত্‌চু চারা খেগ্রিকেংআ
Mátchu chárá khegrikéngá, The *bulls* are fighting.

মেচিকরাং মি সংথকেংআ
Mechikráng mi shangthakengá, The *women* are sifting rice.

আংনি মাআ নও সক্‌বাহা
Angni máá no shakbáhá, My *mother* (and) *sister* have arrived.

বুচুমারাং আগান্‌গ্রিকেংআ
Buchumáráng ágángrikéngá, The old *women* are conversing.

দোবিমা বিসা বদিলেংআ
Dobimá bishá badilengá, The *hen* shelters her young.

মাত্‌চু বিমানি সক গেব্রি
Mátchu bimáni shak gébri, The *cow* has four teats.

চিংনি সারানি বল্ দাল্গিপা বেঃআহা
Chingni sháráni bal dálgipá béháhá, — Our (house) *tree* is broken.

আংনি আথে মাত্বেয়াচিম উয়া গিম্মাহা
Angni áthé mátbéyáchim, uá gimmáhá, — My *dáo* was very sharp, it has become spoiled.

নাংনি খেত্থাল মাতা মা?
Nángni khetthál mátá má? — Is your knife sharp?

উনা থেকাত্চু রংসা অন্বো
Uná thékatchu rangshá anbo, — Give him a *melon.*

Exercise.—3. In Case.

রিসারাং সেথকেংআ
Risharang shethakengá, — The *children* are writing.

মান্দেরাং রেবাহা
Mánderáng rebáhá, — The *men* have come.

মাত্চু খাতাংআহা
Mátchu khátángáhá, — The *cow* fled.

আচাক সিংএংআ
Achák shingengá, — The *dog* is barking.

বিসারাংখো অকামবো
Bishárángkho akámbo, — Call the *children.*

আথেখো রাঃবাহামা?
Athékho rábáhámá? — Did you bring the *dáo?*

দগাখো চিপাহা
Dagákho chipáhá — The *door* was shut.

ওয়ালখো স্কাহামা?
Owálkho shkáhámá? — Have you lit the *fire?*

থচ্রিখো সঃবো
Thachrikho shahbo, — Light the *lamp.*

উয়া মাআ ফাখো মান্দে রাঃআ (Two nouns in apposition.)
Uá máá phákho mánde ráá, He honors mother and *father.*

ফাখো মান্দে রাঃরংআ
Phákho mánde rárangá, He (understood) always honors his *father.*

মি চাঃজক
Mi chájak, (He) has eaten *rice.*

খান্‌চা স্থুয়াহাচিম
Khánchá shuáháchim, The *cloth* had been washed.

আংআ মংমা গনা রেয়াংএংআ
Angá mangmá ganá reyángengá, I am going to kill an *elephant.*

উয়া খেত্‌থালচি বারিং-বায়েংআ
Uá khetthálchi báring-báyengá, He cuts fruit with a *knife.*

বিসারাং বুদুচি মাত্‌চু খাআহা
Bisháráng buduchi mátchu khááhá, The boys bound the cow with a *rope.*

নাআ রুয়াচি আম্বল্ ফিত্‌বো
Naá ruáchi ámbal phitbo, (You) cut wood with an *axe.*

আংআ আত্‌চিলিচি মি রাগেন
Angá átchilichi mi rágen, I will cut paddy with a *sickle.*

সাহেব বিসারাংনা থাংখা অন্নাহা
Sáheb bishárángná thángkhá ánnáhá, The saheb gave money to the *boys.*

ইসল্ মান্দেরাংনা খাসাবেগিপা
Eshal mánderángná kháshábegippá, God loves (or is a lover of) *all men.*

আফা আংনা খানচা রাঃবাগেন
Aphá ángná khánchá ráabágen, Father will bring *me* clothes.

আংনা সাম নাংআচিম
Angná shám nángáchim, — Medicine was necessary for *me.*

দেথাংনা ফিলাক্‌বা খাসারা
Dethángná philákbá kháshárá, — All love their own *sons* (or children.)

ইসলনা ফিলাক্‌বা খেন্‌থকা
Eshalná philákbá khenthaká, — All fear *God.*

বিসারাং স্কুলোনি রেবাহা
Bisháráng shkuloni rebáhá, — The children have come from *school.*

বলোনি বিজাক গাআকা
Baloni bizhák gááká, — The leaf falls from the *tree.*

নাআ বাওনি রেবাহা?
Náá báoni rebáhá? — From *whence* have you come?

নাআ সাওনিখো থাংখা রাঃবার?
Náá sháonikho thángkhá rábárá? — From *whom* have you got money?

আংআ নকোনিখো বাঃরা সিক্‌সা রাঃবাচিম
Angá nakonikho bárá shikshá rábáchim, — I had taken (or took) one cloth from the *house.*

ঊয়া নাংওনিখো মায়খো রাঃআংআ
Uá nángonikho máikho ráhángá? — What did he take from *you?*

আংআ বাজালোনিখো মেরং ব্রেবাহা
Angá bázhálonikho merang brebáhá, — I having bought rice, fetched it from the *bazar.*

নাআ নকোনিখো মায়রাংখো রাবাচিম
Náá nakonikho máirángkho rábáchim? — What (things) did you bring from the *house.*

আংনি খামখো খাগেন Angni khámkho khágen	(I) will do *my* work.
উআ বল্নি বিথে নাম্মা মা? Uá balnibithe námma má?	Is the fruit of that *tree* good?
রামসিংনি মাৎচুরাং সিথক আহা Ramshingni matshuráng shithakáhá	Ramsing's *cattle* have died.
নাংনি জিক্দে নাম্মেংআ Nángni jikdé nammengá?	Is *your* family (lit. wife and son) well?
উনি জিক্নি শা গ্নাং Uni jikni shá gnáng	*His* wife is ill.
সাহেবনি খিতাপ নাম্মা sahebni khitáp námmá	The *saheb's* book is good.
আংনি রেবানিগিমিন মায় অংআহা? A'ngni rebánigimin mái angáhá?	What has resulted from *my* coming?
নকো দংবো Nako dangbo	Remain in the *house*.
আংআ রিংও রেয়াংআহা A'ngá ringo reyángáhá	I went in a *boat*.
জাহাতো নাপে উয়া আন্থাং সংওনা রেয়াংআহা Jáháto nápe uá ántháng shangoná reyángáhá	He went in a *boat to* his own country.
নাংও থাংখা গ্নাং মা? Nángo thángkhá gnáng má?	Have *you* any money?
আংও থাংখা গংবংআ গ্নাং A'ngo thánkho gangbangá gnáng	*I have* five rupees.
উয়া বাজালচি এয়াংআহা Uá bázálchi eyángáhá	He has gone to the *bazar*.

নাআ বাজাল্চিনা এয়াংএ উখো অকাম্বো
Náá bázálchiná eyánge ukho akámbo. — You go to the *bazar* and call him.

ও মান্দেরাং ইবাথক্বো
O! mánderáng ibáthakbo. — *O! men* come.

ও গিত্তেল্ খাশাল্বো
O! Gittel kháshalbo. — *Oh! Lord* have mercy.

II. PRONOUNS.

Ex. Personal Pronouns.

আংআ খিতাপখো ফরায়না আম্মা
A'ngá khitápkho pharáiná ámmá. — *I* can read.

আংআ ববিলখো দক্গ্রিক্গেন
A'ngá babilkho dakgrikgen. — *I* will fight the enemy.

আং বাক্সা দংনা নাংআ
A'ng báksha dangná nángá. — It is right to remain with *me.*

অংখো উয়া খাল্স্থাপাহা
Angkho uá khálsthápáhá. — He blasphemed (or contemned) *me.*

আংনি মাআ ফাআ রেবারা
A'ngni máá pháá rebárá. — *My* parents, (mother and father) have come.

আংনি দেফান্থে নামেদাকে শেআ
A'ngní dephánthe námedáke sheá. — *My* son writes well.

আংনা উয়া উখো অনএনবা রেয়াং-আহা
A'ngná uá ukho anenbá reyáng-áhá. — Having given it to *me*, he went away.

আংনা নাম্মেন খাসাবো
A'ngá námmen khásháb0.

Love *me* very much.

আংনা গুরে মাংসা নাংআ
A'ngná gure mángshá nángá. — A horse is necessary for *me.*

আংনা স্খিগিপা রেবাএংআ
A'ngná skhigipá rebáengá. — A teacher is coming for *me.*

আংওনি আনচি গাআকা
A'ngoni ánchi gááká. — Blood is falling from *me*.

আংওনিখো উখো রিম্মাংআহা
A'ngonikho ukho rimmángáhá. — He was taken away from *me*.

আংও মামুংবা গ্রি
A'ngo mámungbá gri. — I have nothing (lit. nothing is *in me*.)

আংওনা ইবাবো
A'ngoná ibábo. — Come to *me*.

আংচিনা নিবো
A'ngchiná nibo. — Look toward me.

নাআ মিরাংখো চাআহা মা?
Náá mirangkho chááhá má? — Have *you* eaten?

নাআরা ইয়াংনা নাংআ
Náárá iyángná nángá. — *You* must go.

নাআ মায়না ইয়াংখুজা?
Náá máiná iyángkhujá. — Why did *you* not go?

নাংনা মায়খো নাংআ?
Nángná máikho nángá? — What do *you* want?

উয়া নাংনা উখো অন্না নাংগেন
Uá nángná ukho anná nánggen. — He must give it to *you*.

নাংওনি মায় গাআকা?
Nángoni mái gááka? — What has fallen from *you*?

চাউগিপা উখো নাংওনিখো রাসেকাহামা?
Cháugipá ukho nángonikho rásheká-hámá? — Did the thief take that from *you*?

নাংনি সা মায়খায়ে দংআ?
Nángni shá máikháié dangá? — How are *you*? Lit. what is the state of *your* illness?

নাংনি নাম্মেন দুঃখ অংআমা?
Nángni námmen dukḥ angámá? — Have *you* much distress?

উয়া নাংনি সাখো নাম্মাতখেন
Uá nángni shákho námmátkhen. — He will cure *you*.

আংআ নাংওনা ইবাগেন
A'ngá nángoná ibágen. — I will come *to you*.

উয়া নাংবাকসা ইয়াংআহা
Uá nángbákshá iyángáhá. — He went with *you*.

সাহেব নাংনি গিমিন ইনোনা ইবাএংআ
Sáheb nángni gimin inoná ibáengá. — The saheb has come here on *your* account.

আঙা নাঙনি আসেল্ মাইখো খাগেন?
A'ngá nángni áshel máikho khágen? — What will I do for *you*?

উয়া নাম্মেন নাম্মা।
Uá námmen námmá. — *He* is very good.

উয়া নাম্মেন বিমচিপে গামেংআ।
Uá námmen bimchipe gámengá. — *He* is working very industriously.

উয়া আংখো খাল্স্থাপা।
Uá ángkho khálsthápá. — *He* ridicules me.

উয়ান নাংখোন্ নিক্খুজা।
Uán nángkhon nikkhujá. — *He* has not seen you.

উখো আংআ নিকাহা।
Ukho ángá nikáhá. — I saw *him*.

উয়াখো ওয়াত্বো।
Uákho oátbo. — Send *him*.

উখোন আকামেন্বা ইবাখুজা।
Ukhon ákámenbá ibákhujá. — Having called *her* (she) did not come.

উখো রাংবো।
Ukho rángbo. — Take *it* away.

উখো আংআ দামরাওনা রাআংআহা।
Ukho ángá Dámráoná ráángáhá. — I took *it* away to Damra.

উনা অন্বো।
Uná anbo. — Give (it) to *him*.

মেম্সাহেব্ উনা খাসারা।
Memsháheb uná kháshará. — The lady loves *her*.

উনা খিতাপ্ দংআ।
Uná khitáp dangá. — There is a book for *him*.

উওনি আংআ রেবারা।
Uoni ángá rebárá. — I came from *him*.

উওনিখো রাঃবাবো।
Uonikho rahbábo. — Bring (it) from *him*.

উনি ফাআ ইবায়েংআ।
Uni pháá ibáyengá. — *His* father is coming.

উনি নক দাল্বেয়া।
Uni nak dálbeyá. — *His* house is very large.

উনি রেবাখো উইমেন্বা আন্সেংআহা।
Uni rebáko uienbá (anga) ánshengáhá. — Knowing *his* coming (I) was happy.

উনি আগানাখো খ্নাএমু, আং খেন্জক
Uni ágánákho knáemu áng khenjak. — Having heard *his* speech, I feared.

আংআ উনি গিমিন ইনোনা ইবাহা
A'ngá uni gimin inoná ibáhá. — On account of *him* I came here.

উও মায় গ্নাং?
Uo mái gnáng? — What has *he?* (lit. what is in *him?*)

উওচাচা নাম্মেদাকে খাবো
Uochách́á nammedáke khábo, — Like *him*, do well.

চিংআ রেনা স্কা
Chingá rená shká. — *We* wish to go.

চিংআ রেনা আমজা
Chingá rená ámjá. — *We* cannot go.

নাসিমাং চিংখো অকামাহামা?
Náshimáng chingkho akámáhámá? — Did *you* call *us*.

নাআমাং চিংবাকসা ইয়াংগেনমা?
Náámáng chingbáksh́á iyánggenmá? — Will *you* go with *us*.

চিংনা নাআমাংখো অকামাতাহা
Chingná náámángkho akámátáhá. — *You* were called for *us*.

চিওনি নাআমাংওনা উয়া ইয়াং ফিলবো
Chingoni náámángoná uá iyáng-philbo. — He returned to *you* from *us*.

আচিংওনিখো রাসেকে নাসিমাংখো অননাহা
A'chingonikho rásheke náshimánkho annáhá. — Having taken (it) from *us* (he) gave it to *you*.

আচিংনি গামদ্রাংখো রাসেকাংআহা
A'chingni gámdrángkho ráshekángáhá. — *Our* property was stolen (looted.)

চিংওনা ইবাবো
Chingoná ibábo. — Come to *us* (lit. in our direction.)

নাসিমাং চিংনি খাথাখো উইয়ামা?
Náshimáng chingni khátákho uiámá? — Have *you* understood *us.?*

উয়ামাং নাসিমাংখো উইয়ানা আমজা
Uámáng náshimángkho uiáná ámjá. — *They* are not able to understand you.

উয়ামাদাংখো নাসিমাংনা মেসাকগেন
Uámádángkho náshimángná meshakgen. — (I) will show *them* to you.

বিসারাং উয়ামাদাংওনি খাতাংআহা
Bishárang uámádángoni khátángáhá. — The children fled from *them*.

মান্দেরাং উয়ামাদাংওনিখো মিরং চাউআংআহা Mánderáng uámádángonikho mirang cháuángáhá.	The men stole rice from *them.*
উয়ামাদাংনি মাত্চুরাং নাম্জা Uámádángni mátchuráng námjá.	*Their* cattle are bad.
আংআ উয়ামাংনি নামগিজাখো উইয়া A'ngá uámángni námgijákho uiyá.	I know *their* bad conduct.
আংআ উয়ামাদাংনি নাম্মা খাম্খো নিকে নাম্নিকাহা A'ngá uámádángni námmá khámkho nike námnikáhá.	I was pleased at seeing *their* good work.
উয়ামাদাংও অনথিসা মিরং গ্নাংমা? Uámádángo anthishá miráng gnángmá?	Have *they* any rice?
বাও, উয়ামাদাংও নাম্মেন দুঃখ অংএংআ Bao, uámádángo námmen dukh angengá.	No, *they* have great distress.
বাসাকো উয়ামাদাংও মিরং অংগেন? Básháko uámádángo mirang angen?	When will *they* have rice?
সাল্খলাত্চিও উয়ামাংও মিরং বাংবেগেন Shálkhalátchio uámángo mirang bángbegen.	In thirty days *they* will have plenty of rice.

Ex. 2. Other Pronouns.

জে রেবাগিপা উয়া বিসাখো রিম্বাজক Je rebágippá uá bishákho rimbájak.	The *one who* came brought the child.
জেখো নাআ নিক্গেন ukho ওয়াতাত্বো Jekho náá nikgen ukho ouátátbo.	*Send whom* you will see.
জেচি উয়া ইয়া খামদাকাহা, উখো আংনা মেসকবো Jechi uá iá khámdákáhá ukho ángná meshakbo.	Show me that with which he did this (work.)
জেনা নাআ উখো আন্নাহা উয়া বাওনা রেবারা? Jená náá ukho onnáhá uá baoná rebárá?	*He to whom* you gave it, where has he gone?
জেওনি উয়া ফাইসা গাআকজক উনা অনফিলবো Jeoni uá pháishá gáákjak uná anphilbo.	Return that pice to him from whom it fell.

জেওনিখো সিফাহিরাং মিরংখো রাঃসে-কাংআহা উয়ামাংনা থাংখা অন্না নাংআ Jeonikho shipáhiráng mirangkho rah̤shekángáhá uámángná thánká anná nángá.	Those from whom the sepoys took rice, to them money ought to be given.
জেরাংনি খিতাপ গ্নাং উয়ারাং ইবাথকচিনা Jerangni khitáp gnáng, uáráng ibáthakchiná.	Let *those who* have books come.
জেও মান্দেরাং দংরংআ, উয়া বিয়াপনি বিমুং সং Jeo mánderáng dangrangá, uá biyápni bimung shang.	The name of the *place where* people dwell is village, (or city.)
জেও থাংখা দংআ, উখো ওয়াত্‌বো Jeo thángkhá dangá ukho oatbo.	Send *him who* has money.

উয়া আচাক সাওনি? Uá áchák sháoni?	Whose dog is *that?*
ইয়া মান্দেনি Iá mándeni.	*This* man's.
উনোনা এয়াংএনবা ইয়া আথেচি উয়া বল্‌খোসা দেন্‌বো Unoná eyángenbá iá áthechi uá balkhoshá denbo.	Go *there* (that place) and cut *that* tree with *this* dáo.
গিপিনখোসা অকাম্‌বো Gipinkhoshá akámbo.	Call *another.*
আংআ মামুংখোবা নিক্‌জাজক A'ngá mámungkhobá nikjájak.	I did not see *any one.*
সাকান্‌থিনা থাংখা সংসাখো অন্নাহা Shákánthiná thángkhá shangshákho annábá.	(I) gave to *each,* one rupee.
ইন্দিগিতা এবারা Indigitá ebárá.	*So many* come.
জেগিতা নাংবাকসা ইয়াংজক উয়ামাং-না খাসানা নাংআ Jegitá nángbáksha iyángjak uámángná kháshánä nángá.	*As many as* went with you, those you ought to love.
ইয়া মেদিকো চিখো অন্‌বো Iá mediko chikho anbo.	Put water in *this* vessel.

উয়া চি খাসিন Uá chi kháshin.	*That* water is cold.
নাআ মামুংখোবা আগানাবে Náá mámungkhobá ágánábe.	Do not you tell *any one.*
আঙ্আ ইয়া শিলায়চি উয়া মাপিল্ দকে গাল্লাহা A'ngá iá shiláichi uá mápil dake gálláhá.	I killed *that* bear with *this* gun.

III. ADJECTIVES.

বিয়াপ নাম্মা Biyáp námmá.	A *good* place.
নক্ নামজা Nak námjá.	A *bad* house.
উয়া আব্রি চুআ Uá ábri chuá.	That mountain is *high.*
উয়া চিআখল থুআ Uá chiákhal thuá.	That hole of water is *deep.*
চিরিংনি চি খাসিনা Chiringni chi kháshiná.	The water of the spring is *cold*
মেচিক খ্নি, গ্নাং নিথোআ Mechik khni gnáng nithoá.	A long haired woman is *handsome.*
খিলদিংনি বাঃরা বকা Khildingni báḥrá baká.	Cloth of cotton thread is *white.*
চেং মেসেংআ Cheng mishengá.	The tamarind is *sour.*
থেরিক চিয়া Thérik chiá.	The plantain is *sweet.*
জালিক সাআ Jálik sháá.	Pepper is *sharp tasted.*
নিম বিথে খাঃআ Nim bithé kháḥá.	The fruit of the *neem* is *bitter.*
রো নাথক চানা থোআ Ró náthak chána thoá.	The *roh* fish is *good* to eat.

উনি গুরেনা বাতে নাংনি গুরে গংরাক্ বাতা Uni gurená báté nángni guré gangrákbátá.	Your horse is *faster* than his!

উয়া মংমানা বাতে ইয়া মংমা দাল্‌বাতা Uá mangmáná báte iá mangmá dálbátá.	This elephant is *larger* than that.
আংনি আচাকনা বাতে উনি আচাক নামবাতা A'ngni áchákná báte uni áchák námbátá.	His dog is *better* than mine.
আংনা বাতে নাআ উইয়া A'ngná báte náá uiyá.	You are wiser than I.
দখ্রুনা বাতে দোখা দাল্‌বাতা Dakhruná bátė dokhá dálbátá.	The crow is larger than the sparrow.
মাপুল্‌না বাতে মাত্‌চা রাক্‌বাতা Mápulná báté mátchá rákbátá.	The tiger is *stronger* than the bear.
মেচিকনা বাতে মেয়াসা রাক্‌বাতা Mechikná báte meyáshá rákbátá.	Man is *stronger* than woman.
বিসানা বাতে ফান্থে উইবাতা Bisháná báte phánthe uibátá.	The young man *knows more* than the child.
বিসারাংনি গিসেপো উয়া নামবাতা Bishárángni gishepo uá námbátá.	He is the *best* of the boys.
আচিকরাংনি গিসেপো নাআ দালবাতা Achikrángni gishepo náá dálbátá.	You are *greatest* among the Garos.
দারাংনি গিসেপো ইয়া চন্‌বাতা Dárángni gishepo iá chanbátá.	Among all, this is the *least*.
মাত্‌বুরুংনি গিসেপো মংমা দাল্‌বাতা Mátburungni gishepo mang dálbátá.	The elephant is the *largest* of jungle beasts.
আব্রিরাংনি জাত্‌চিও উয়া আব্রি চুবাতা A'brirángni játchio uá ábri chubátá.	That is the *highest* of the mountains.
বলরাংনি গিসেপো ফ্রাপ দাল্‌বাতা Balrángni gishepo phráp dálbátá.	Among trees the pepul is *largest.*

মান্দে সাকচিবংআ নক রিকেংআ Mándé shákchibangá nak rikéngá.	*Fifty* men are building a house.
বিসা খল্‌গ্রিক স্খুলোনি রেয়াংআহা Bishá khalgrik shkhuloni réyángáhá.	*Twenty* boys came from school.
নাথক মাংদক রাঃবাবো Náthak mángdak ráhbábo.	Bring *six* fishes.

থাংখা সত্বংআ অন্না আম্গেন্মা ?
Thángkhá shathbangá anná ámgenmá?

Will not *fifty* rupees be given? (lit. will I not get?)

আচাক মাংগ্নিখো দকে গাল্লাহা
A'chák mánggnikho daké gálláhá.

Two dogs were killed.

মংমা মাংচিবংআ মবায়েংআ
Mangmá mángchibangá mabáyéngá.

Fifteen elephants are being brought.

ফায়েসা গান্দাবৃচি দোচি খলগ্রিক মান্না
Pháyéshágándábrichi dochi khalgrik mánná.

With *four* pice *twenty* eggs are got.

দোবিসা মাংচিদকখো দোরেং বাল্লাংআহা
Dobishá mángchidakkho doreng bállángáhá.

The hawk carried away *sixteen* chickens.

মান্দে সাকসা স্লায়চি মাতচা মাংচেত্ গআহা
Mándé shákshá shlásychi mátchá mángchet gaáhá.

One man killed *eight* tigers with a gun.

উনো মাত্চু সত্বি গ্নাং
Uno mátchu shatbri gnáng.

Forty cattle are there.

দবক মাংগ্নি ব্রেবাবো
Dabak mánggni brebábo.

Buy and bring *two* goats.

বাঃরা সিক্চিখুংখো সুনা রাঃআংবো
Báḥrá shikchikungkho shuná ráḥángbo.

Wash and bring *ten pieces* of cloth.

জাচিগ্নিও বিলসিসা অংআ
Jáchignio bilshishá angá.

In *twelve* months is *one* year.

বিলসি রিত্চাসা থাংগিপা মান্দে বাংজা
Bilshi ritcháshá thánggipá mánde bángjá.

Centenarians are *scarce.*

IV. VERBS.

Ex. 1. Simple Verbs.

বিসারাং মি চাঃআ
Bisháráng mi cháḥá.

The children eat *(rice.)*

মেচিক্রাং রেখা সেয়া
Mechikráng rékhá shéyá.

The girls *write.*

উয়ামাং নাথক রিঃমা
Uámáng náthak riḥmá. — they *catch* fish.

মাত্চু সাম চা.আ
Mátchu shám cháḥá. — The cow *eats* grass.

উয়ামাং মেরং রাবায়েংআ
Uámáng mérang rábáyengá. — They are *bringing* rice.

মেচিকরাং মি সংএংআ
Mechikráng mi shangengá. — The women are *sifting* rice.

মান্দেরাং নক রিকেংআ
Mánderáng nak rikéngá. — The men are *building* a house.

উয়া দারিয়াংএংআ
Uá dáriyángéngá. — He is *running*.

মিসারি মিন্জক, উয়া রানা নামাহা
Mishári minjak, uá ráná námáhá. — The paddy *has ripened.* It *has become fit* to cut.

উয়ামাং ইয়ানোনি রেয়াংজক
Uámáng iyánoni réyángjak. — They *went* from here,

মান্দেরাং সক্বাজক
Mándéráng shakbájak. — The people *have arrived.*

উয়ামাংনি খাম অংআহা
Uámángni khám angáhá. — Their work has *been* finished.

উয়া নক্চি রেয়াংআহা
Uá nakchi reyángáhá. — He *went* to the house.

উয়ামাংনি দেফান্থে দেমিচিক গ্রিচিম
Uámángni dephánthe demichik grichim. — They *were* childless.

চিংআ মি চাঃআহাচিম
Chingá mi cháḥáháchim. — We *had eaten.*

নাসিমাং রেয়াংআচিম উওন আং অকাম্জক
Náshimáng reyangáchim uon áng akámjak. — You *had gone;* then I called (you.)

সাহেব ফরায়েআচিম উওন আগানাহা
Sáheb pharáieachim uon ágánáhá, — Saheb *had read,* then spoke.

আচিংআ উনোন দংআচিম
A'chingá unon dangáchim. — We *remained* (dwelt) there.

উয়ামাদাং ইবাএংআহা Uámádáng ibáéngábá.	They *were coming.*
বিসারাং আগানগ্রিকেংআচিম Bisháráng ágánárikéngáchim.	The children *were talking.*
মাত্চরাং সংওনা রেবাএংআচিম Mátchuráng shangoná rébáengáchim.	The cattle *were going* to the village.
আংআ এবাএংআচিম উওন নাংখো গ্রংজক A'ngá ébánégáchim, uon nángkho grangjak.	I *was coming,* then I met you.
মান্দেবিসারাং নকো নাপেংআচিম Mándébisháráng nako nápengáchim.	The boys *were entering* the house.
স্খিগিপারাং স্খিয়েআচিম Shkhigipáráng shkhiyéngáchim.	The teachers *were teaching.*
আং সেআএংআচিম, উনজামানো ইবাজক A'ng sheáengáchim, unjámáno ibájak.	I *had been writing,* afterwards came.
সাহেবখো নিনা ইন্নে ইবাএংআচিম Sáhebkho niná inne ibáengáchim.	I *was coming* to see the Saheb.

নাআ জেখো দাকগেন. আংআবা ডখোন দাক্গেন্ Náá jekho dákgen, ángábá ukhon dákgen.	I also *will do* that which you *will do.*
স্খাং দুঃখ খাওদে জামানো সুখ মানগেন্ Shkháng dukḥ kháode jámáno shukh mángen.	If at first distress is felt, afterwards happiness *will be experienced.*
খাসাগিপানাসা ফিলাক্বা খাসাগেন Khásházgipánáshá philákbá khásházgen,	All *will love* one who loves (or a lover.)
মংমাখো আরিকবো, উয়া খাত্নিম Mangmákho árikbo uá khátnim.	Drive off the elephant. It *will flee.*
আংআ সাক্সান্বা রেয়াংনা খেন জাওয়া Angá shákshánbá reyángná khenjáoá.	I *will not fear* to go alone.
উয়া জেখো দাকবো ইন্গেন্ উখোন দাক্গিনক্ Uá jekho dákbo ingen, ukhon dákginak.	I *will do,* or am ready to do, that which he says.

থল্লে আগানগিপাখো, ঈসল নরকো গাল্‌খেন Thalle ágángippákho Eshal narako gálkhen.	God *will cast* the liar into hell.
আংআ মাতচাখো স্লুচি গনিম্‌ A'ngá mátchákho shlychi ganim.	I *will shoot* a tiger with a gun.
নাংনি আচাক্‌ বিসাখো আংআ রাহংনক Nángni áchák bisbákho ángá ráhangnak.	I *will bring* your puppy.
সাল্‌গ্নি সালগিথাম রেয়াংওদে জা গিতাল নাগেন্‌ Shalgni shálgithám reyángode jágitál nágen,	In two or three days the new moon *will rise*.

নাআ খামখাএ আংনি নকোনা রেবাবো Náá khámkháe ángni nakoná rebábo.	Having done your work *come* to my house.
বিম্‌চিপে রেখা স্খিচিনা নাআ উখো আগানবো Bimchipe rekhá shkhichiná náá ukho áganbo.	*Bid* (them) to study with energy.
থল্লে দাআগান্নে বিসারাংখো বেংবো Thalle dáaganne bisharángkho bengbo.	*Forbid* the children to lie.
নখলরাং গিতেলনি গেয়েতাগিতা গামচিনা Nakhalráng gitelni geyetágitá gámchiná.	*Let* servants work according to the commands of the master.
মেচিক্‌রাং সেনি নামনিকাখো দাক্‌চং Mechikráng sheni námnikákho dákchang.	*Let* women be subject to their husbands.

মান্দেরাং নাথক রিম্‌না রেয়াংআহা mánderáng náthak rimná reyángáhá.	The men have gone *to catch* fish.
বিসারাং মংমা নিনা রেবায়েংআও আংআ গ্রংজক Bisháráng mangmá niná rebáyengáo ángá granjak.	I met the children in (their) coming *to see* the elephant.

উয়া মাআ ফাআখো গ্রংনাইন্নে নক্চি রেয়াংগেন
Uá máá pháákho grangnáinne nakchi reyánggen.
He will go home *to meet* his parents.

সাগিপানা সাম অন্নাইন্নে ওজা রেবাহা
Shágipáná shám annáinne ozhá rebáhá.
The doctor came to *give* medicine to the sick (man.)

উয়ামাংনি খামখো নিকোদে নাসিমাং উইনা মান্‌গেন
Uámángni khámkho nikode náshimáng uiná mángen.
You may know them by *seeing* (if you see) their work.

নাআ রেয়াংওদে সংনি মান্দেরাং নাম্‌নিক্‌গেন
Náá reyángode shangni mánderáng námnikgen.
If you go, the villagers will be pleased.

গিসিকো জাগ্রেংওদে নাম্মা খামখো খানা আমজা
Gishiko jágrengode námmá khámkho khánná ámjá.
Being disturbed in mind one can not do good work.

চাউগিপা চাউনা রেবায়েংআচিম, আংখো নিকোয়া খাতাংআহা
Cháugipá cháuná rebáengáchim, ángkho nikoá khátángáhá.
The thief was coming to steal, *seeing* me he fled.

দেগিপা গ্রাপেংআচিম, ফানি সক্‌বাওয়া থিপাহা
Degipá grápengáchim, pháni shakbáoá thipáhá.
The son was crying, father *arriving*, he ceased.

বল্লোনি অংউনোআ মাত্‌চা উখো রিম্মাহা
Baloni angunoá mátchá ukho rimmáhá.
Descending from the tree, a tiger seized him.

সাহেব ইনোনা রেবাওআ কলিকাতাও সাল্‌চিখুং দংআহা
Shaheb inoná rebáoá kolikátáo shálchikhung dangáhá.
The saheb *in coming* here, spent ten days in Calcutta.

উনি আরাতাখো নিকে ফিলাক্‌বা উনা খাসাজা
Uni árátákho nik philákbá uná kháshájá.
Having seen his idledess no one likes him.

রামাও মাত্চা গ্নাং ইন্নাখো খ্নায়ে
আংআ ফিল্বাহা
Rámáo mátchá gnáng innákho — *Having heard* that there is a tiger in the road, I returned.

দাওবিল্সি মি বাংএ মানেন্বা নাআবা
খাত্চাবেয়াহা
Dáobilshi mi bánge mánenbá náábá khátchábeyáhá. — *Having got* much rice this year you were very happy.

নাংনি অকুমু চাকাখো নিকেন্বা আং-
আ নাংনা খাসাবেজক
Nángni akumu chákákho nikenbá ángág náná kháshábejak. — *Having seen* your fasting I was much pleased with you.

Exercise 2. Compound Verbs.

উয়া নকচি রেয়াংএ রেবাফিলাহা
Uá nakchi reyángé rébáphiláhá. — He having gone to the house *returned.*

নাংনি খিথাপরাংখো রাঃবাফিল্বো
Nángni khithápránkho ráḫbáphilbo. — *Bring back* your books.

আংআ সাক্সান রেয়াংনা খেন্নে
ফিল্বাজক্
A'ngá shákshán reyángná khenne philbájak. — Fearing to go alone, I *returned.*

খ্নাআংআচিম
আচিক্রাং খান্চা ব্রেনা রেবাথায়াহা
A'chingráng kháncbá brená rebá-thááhá — The Garos *came again* to buy cloth.

আংনি উখো রেবাবো ইন্নাখো নাআবা
খ্নাআংআচিম
A'ngni ukho rebábo innákho náábá khnángáchim. — Heaving heard my command to him to come, you came.

নাংনি মংমা নিক্বাখো আরিকনা
মান্দে রিমচিমুবো
Nángni mangmá nikbákho árikaná, mánde rimchimubo. — Collect men to drive off the elephant that you saw.

ফানি রেবাখো খ্নাসয়ে দেদ্রাং
খাত্চাজক
Pháni rébákho khnáshayé dedráng khátchájak. — Having heard before of the arrival of the father, the sons rejoiced.

বিসারাং সক্বামান্নো মি সংথকেংআ
Bishárang shakbámánno mi shang-thakéngá. — Before the arrival of the children the rice was being cleaned.

উয়া বাজালো থাংখা গুয়াল্‌বায়ে ফিলাংআহা
Uá bázálo thángkhá guálbáiyé philángáhá.

Having forgotten his money in the bazar, he *went back.*

আংআ উনি গ্রখো চতাহাচিম, ইন্দিদে মায়না জানাপা?
A'ngá uni grakho chatáháchim, indidé máiná jánápá?

I have paid his debt, then why does he *reassert it?*

নাংনি মাচ্চু রাআ নামজা, ওয়াল্‌ফিল্‌বো
Nángni Mátchu rábá námjá, oálphilbo.

Your taking the cow was not good; *give it back.*

গিসিক গ্রিপা মান্দে মামুংখো দাক্‌নাবা চলজক্
Gishik gripá mándé mámungkho dáknábá chaljak.

The ignorant man *is not fit* to to do any work.

আচিক সংওনা সাহেব রেরুরাবারাংআ, উখো গ্রাংজামা
A'chik shangoná sháheb rerurábárángá ukho grangjámá.

The Saheb *comes again and again* to the Garo country; have you not met him?

মান্দেসাল মান্দেআসেল নাংওবা জাজ্রেংজা
Mándéshál mándé áshel nángobá jájréngjá.

In the presence of wise men, you *are not thoughtful.*

মেংগ রেবায়েংআচিম আচাক্‌না খেন্নে খাত্‌ফিলাংআহা
Menga rebáyengáchim, ácháknа́ khénné khátphilángáhá.

The cat was coming, but fearing the dog *fled away (back.)*

মাত্‌চা মাত্‌চুখো চিক্‌মানো দবক্‌খোবা চিক্‌থায়েজক
Mátchá mátchukho chikmáno dabakkhobá chikthaiejak.

The tiger after killing the cow, killed the goat also.

সিগিমিন মান্দেখো থাংচাআত্‌না ফিলক্‌বা আমজা
Shigimin mándékho thángcháátná philakbá ámjá.

None are able *to cause* the dead to *live again.*

ইয়া আথেখো আংআ রাহাআহা, মাত্‌জাওদে অন্‌ফিল্‌গেন
Iyá áthékho ángá ráháhá, mátjáodé anphilgen.

I brought this dao, if it is not sharp *will return* it.

উয়া সং নিক্‌খুজা নাআ উখো রিমাংবো
Uá shang nikkhujá, náá ukho rimángbo.

(I) have not seen that country, you take him.

আংআ সংচি রেয়াংওদে নাংনি নকোবা নাপাংগেন A'ngá shangchi réyángodé nángni nakobá nápánggen.	If I go to the village I *will enter* your house.
উখো মিথেলা ফিলাক্‌চিন খ্নাসেং-আংআহা Ukho mithelá philákchin khnásheng-ángáhá.	His praise *has spread* every where.
ফ্রিংও নাআ চাখাত্‌বাবো উওদে উখো গ্রুংগেন Phringo náá chákhátbábo, uodé ukho grangen.	*Having risen* in the morning *come*, then you will meet him.
উয়া খিথাপ নাম্মারাংখো সেয়ে রাঃআংজক Uá khitháp námmárángkho sheyé ráḥángjak	He *selected and took away* good books.

V. ADVERBS.

ইন্দাকে মংমা দাল্লাখো আংআ ফাংনাবা নিক্‌খুজা Indáké mangmá dallákho ángá phángnábá nikkhujá.	So large an elephant as this I have *never* seen.
উয়ামাং গোয়ালপারাওনা বাসাকো রেবাগেন Uámáng Goalpáráoná básháko rebágen?	*When* will they come to Gowalpara?
আংআ কলিকাতাখো চাংসাবা নিক্‌খুজা A ngá Kalikátákho chángshábá nikkhujá.	I have *never once* seen Calcutta.
ইয়া সংনি মেচিক্‌রাং স্খাংও রেখা স্খিজাচিম্‌ Iyá shangni mechikráng skhángo rekhá skhijáchim.	The women of this country had not before learned to read and write.
ঈসল ফিলাক্‌খোন নিকা, ফিলাকোন গ্নাং Ishal philákhon niká, philákon gnáng.	God sees all, is *everywhere*.

উখো ইনোনা রেবাচিনা নাআ আগানাত্‌বো Ukho inoná rebáchiná náá ágánátbo.	You tell him to come here.
নাসিমাং ইনোনি বাওনা রেয়াংগেন Náshimáng inoni báoná reyánggen?	*Where* will you go from *here?*
মাত্‌চুরাংখো আফাল্‌চি আরিকাত্‌বো Mátchurángkho áphálchi árikátbo.	Drive the cows *out.*
বিসারাংখো নক্‌নিংচি রিমাংবো Bishárángkho nakningchi rimángbo.	Bring the children *within* the house.
রামাও মাত্‌চা গ্নাং, গিসিক রাকে রেয়াংবো Rámáo mátchá gnáng, gishik ráke reyángbo.	There is a tiger in the road, go carefully.
নাআ উখো মল্‌মলে রিমবাবো, উওদে রেবাগেন Náá ukho malmale rimbábo uode rebágen.	Bring him *gently,* then he will come.
উখো মি বাক্‌ ২ সংচিন ইন্‌বো, অখ্রিবেয়াহা Ukho mi bákbák shangchin inbo akhribeyáhá.	Tell him to cook the rice quickly, I am very hungry.
থল্লে আগানা নাম্‌জা, উনিগিমিন বেবে আগানবো Thalle ágáná námjá, unigimin bebe áganbo.	To speak *falsely* is wicked. therefore speak *truthfully.*
গংরাকে রেয়াংবো, খাসিনে রেয়াংওদে সাল্‌নিগেন Gongráke reyángbo, kháshine reyángode shálnigen.	Go *rapidly.* If you go *slowly* night will come.
নাম্মেদাকে গামোদে ফিলাকান নামনিকা Námmedáke gámode philákán námniká.	If you work *well,* all are pleased.

VI. INDECLINABLE WORDS.

আংনি মিখাংওনা রেবাবো A'ngni mikhángoná rebábo.	Come *to* me.
উনি মিখাংওনি রেয়াংবো Uni mikhángoni reyángbo.	Go *from* him.

নক্‌চিন রেয়াংজক Nakchin reyángjak.	(He) went *to* (towards) the house.
নক্‌নি নিংও রিমাংআহা Nakni ningo rimángáhá.	(He) was taken *into* the house.
নক্‌নি নিংওনিখো উখো রিমাংজক Nakni ningonikho ukho rimángjak.	He was taken out *from* the house.
আংনি আসেল উয়া খামখো খাগেন মা? A'ngni áshel uá khámkho khágen má?	Will you do that work *for* me ?
আংআ নাংনি বাক্‌সা খাগেন A'ngá nángni bákshá khágen.	I will do (it) *with* you.

For other prepositions, see the prefixes to the cases.

ইনোনা রেবাবো, উনোসা মান্‌গেন Inoshá rebábo, unoshá mángen.	Come here, *then* you will get.
উনিখোয়া উয়া সংওনা রেয়াংজক Unikhoá uá shangoná reyángjak.	*Then*, (after that) he went to the village.
আংআ উনোনা সকাংআহা ইন্দিবা নাংখো গ্রংখুজা A'ngá unoná shakángáhá indibá nángkho grangkhujá.	I arrived there, *but* did not meet you.
সাহেব মেমসাহেব আরো বাবা ইবাখেন Sháheb memsháheb áro bábá ibákhen.	Saheb memshaheb *and* the baba will come.
আংআ আগানা স্কাচিম ইন্দিবা খেনজক A'ngá ágáná shkáchim indibá khenjak.	I wanted to speak *but* feared.

For other conjunctions see table of conjunctions.

For other easy, and more difficult sentences the learner is refered to the Garo First, Second and Third Books.